# THE GILLIGAN VARIATIONS

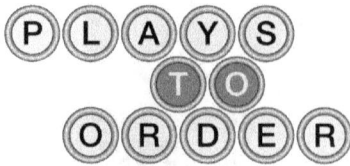

A Plays to Order collection
Published by Plays To Order
5724 Hollywood Blvd., Suite 109
Los Angeles, CA 90028
www.playstoorder.com

First Edition: November 2016

ISBN-13: 978-0-9984173-0-1
ISBN-10: 0-9984173-0-0

Cover design: Sean Abley

# THE GILLIGAN VARIATIONS

## Ten plays inspired by a certain deserted island...

Written by

Sean Abley
Jessica Burton
Liesl Ehmke
Kyle Philip Jackola
Caitlin McCommis
Sean Michael McCord
Kimberly Patterson
Meghan Reimers
Lydia Stewart
Megan Wheelock

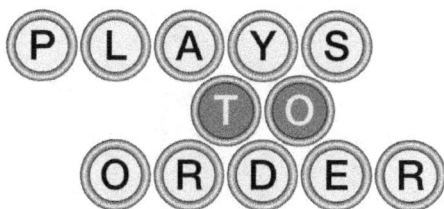

PLAYS
TO
ORDER

# ACKNOWLEDGEMENTS

Many thanks to the Playwrights Lab at Hollins University, program director Todd William Ristau, and our Adaptations professor Megan Gogerty, for the environment, inspiration, and permission to fail spectacularly.

# TABLE OF CONTENTS

# HERE'S WHAT HAPPENED...

In the last week of the summer 2016 semester of the Playwrights Lab at Hollins University, the Adaptations class was given their final writing assignment—adapt the opening credits of *Gilligan's Island* into a short play. (Season One, black and white, Professor and Mary Ann referred to as "...the rest...") Having already adapted two fairy tales, a song, and personal stories shared by fellow classmates, this all-too-familiar theme song and accompanying series' prologue montage provided a unique challenge; should the playwrights pen strict dramatizations of the show's opening, or dig deeper and risk straying too far from the source material to be considered an adaptation?

The resulting ten plays were anything but slavish transcriptions of Sherwood Schwartz and George Wyle's bouncy ode to a fantasy island. Instead, the playwrights served up tales of mystery, murderous spouses, the end of the world, and existential crisis. There was comedy, drama, absurdism, American expressionism, noir, science fiction. Some included fair use-protected versions of the show's characters on a familiar deserted isle; others were so far removed from the source material it took multiple reads to glean the connection. Some were under ten pages; others were pushing thirty. And each was completely different from the rest.

We here at Plays to Order are thrilled to send *The Gilligan Variations* out on its three-hour tour. (And by "we" we mean "me," as in me, Sean Abley, who just so happens to be the publisher and a student in the Adaptations class.) The Playwrights Lab prides itself on the huge amount of material the MFA candidates create while attending the program, and it would be a shame for these fun pieces to get lost in the crowd while waiting for the perfect production opportunity. So they won't!

Enjoy! And please let us know what you think! All the playwrights can be contacted via the Plays to Order webpage—www.playstoorder.com.

Sean Abley
Publisher, Plays to Order
MFA candidate (2017), Playwrights Lab at Hollins University

# ON ADAPTATION

As dramatists, there are two ways we can approach adaptation. We can be diligent translators, capturing the essence of a book (or poem, or hilarious TV series) and sculpting it into a shape suitable for the stage. This method asks us to be precise, to be efficient, and most of all, to be faithful—to the spirit of the original work, if not the every jot and dot of the thing.

The other approach is to be flagrant in our faithlessness; to operate with irreverence and bad manners, to pillage whatever spirit from the original that strikes our fancy and reinvent it as something radically new. With this approach, we are not so much translators as wholly original inventors riffing on a preexisting work and rendering it, perhaps, practically unrecognizable.

We become post-modernists. Like Lichtenstein with his pop art, like Warhol with his soup cans, we take the cultural products of our past and chop them up, rearrange them, and through that violent process, discover something that didn't exist before.

Looking at adaptation through that lens, we are no longer hidebound by narrative. We can adapt anything for the stage. We can adapt flowers. We can adapt dreams. We can adapt pop songs and Post-Its, capitalism and our own beating hearts. If we are ruthless in our reimagination, we can adapt just about anything. Nothing is inherently suitable for the stage, and so everything is. We are free.

Megan Gogerty
Lecturer, University of Iowa Playwrights Workshop
Visiting faculty - Adaptations, Playwrights Lab at Hollins University

# ABOUT THE PLAYWRIGHTS LAB AT HOLLINS UNIVERSITY

Like many of you, I grew up obsessed with *Gilligan's Island*. I had the obligatory crushes on Ginger and Mary Anne, admired the balanced marriage of the Howells, respected the leadership qualities and capacity for empathy of Jonas Grumby, empathized with Gilligan's constant ability to screw things up with the best of intentions, and secretly wanted to be the Professor. I loved the wacky range of characters circulating through that supposedly remote island. I totally understood the euphemism of a "three-hour tour" for something that ended up lasting a life-time instead of being a mere distraction.

Though not a scientist who can make nearly anything out of a couple of coconuts, I did eventually become a professor. In high school when I started doing theatre, I thought it would be just a distracting hobby, but it has become very much a "three-hour tour." There is no leaving that metaphorical island for me, and like the castaways in those sequel movies, I realize now that I don't really want to be anywhere else.

In 2007, I created the graduate program in playwriting at Hollins University, the Playwright's Lab. It is, in my unbiased opinion, the best place in the world to study playwriting. Over the past ten years we have fostered some pretty amazing writers, all highly committed to a lifetime of improving their art, putting what they've learned into action so they can share their work with audiences and learn some more. Hollins playwrights don't sit around waiting to be rescued—I mean, discovered. At Hollins, we get work done. They don't wait for permission or seek validation, they are in too big a hurry to just do stuff!

*The Gilligan Variations* is a perfect example of that philosophy. You have a great teacher who gives an exciting assignment and the students don't see it as a hoop to jump through so they can be validated, they see it as a prompt to learn to be their best by doing their best work, even in class. And then those students, who make up a really supportive community of collaborators rather than a cutthroat environment of competitors, conspire together to share that work with others—even a class exercise. We've had lots of plays come out of the classroom that weren't simply submitted for a grade, but also submitted to publishers, contests and literary offices. I don't know of any other playwriting program that has had nearly as much work go straight from the classroom to the stage and/or publisher.

What makes our program so unique? Well, first of all, it is a high-intensity, low-residency program where you come to Hollins for six-week sessions each summer until you fill up the 60 credit hours and write your thesis play. You decide how fast or how slow you want to take that journey. Some students do two classes a summer and graduate in 6 or 7 summers. Some do four classes a session with a couple of independent studies and graduate in 3 summers. Most do it in 4 summers.

What really sets us apart from most low-residency programs, though, is that we are a micro-brewed immersive theatre experience in cooperation with actual theatre artists and not primarily correspondence based. When we say high intensity, we aren't kidding. When you arrive for your first summer, you're going to be taking a course in playwriting fundamentals with me, along with our signature course, Playwright's Lab. In Lab, each Monday you get to hear a talk given by a prominent theatre artist about their life in the theatre (and they often give a master class over the weekend) with a Q&A to follow. Past guests read like a Who's Who of new play development—folks like Morgan Jenness, Mac Wellman, Todd London, Naomi Wallace, Tanya Saracho, and many others. On Wednesday nights you'll listen to a reading of an early draft of a play by one of your peers with moderated feedback. You're also going to be taking Playscript Analysis, a deep dive into how plays work taught by a guest faculty member. Some of our regular visiting faculty include working professionals like Bonnie Metzgar, Bob Moss, Ruth Margraff, Carl Hancock Rux, Art Borreca, and of course, Megan Gogerty.

In addition to your classes, we encourage our playwrights to be interdisciplinary, and to act in each other's readings, or even direct them. So, all our playwrights are strongly encouraged to attend and participate in the Unified Local Auditions we do at the beginning of each summer. Local community theatre actors and directors from all our regional theatre companies participate alongside our own student playwrights, directors and actors. There is no town and gown separation. The auditions last the whole weekend and are held at Mill Mountain Theatre, which is our local Equity playhouse and collaborative partner.

Every Friday Night we have No Shame Theatre, a venue for the presentation of short, original theatre pieces which our playwrights put up themselves in front of an enthusiastic live audience providing excellent experiential learning opportunities.

Halfway through the summer we fully produce a 24-hour play festival called Overnight Sensations, with six original ten-minute plays written and performed in 24 hours on the main stage of Mill Mountain Theatre to capacity crowds.

At the end of each summer, we have a three-day festival of ten staged readings by our playwrights on Mill Mountain Theatre's Waldron Stage, with a dozen theatre professionals as guest respondents. Past guests have included the lead drama critic from the Chicago Tribune, artistic directors, literary managers, dramaturgs, professional actors, scenic designers, graphic illustrators, Broadway producers, and lots of other representatives of the kinds of collaborators our students might end up working with in the profession. We usually select two of those readings as fully produced workshops at Mill Mountain Stage in the Spring as part of our Hollins-Mill Mountain Festival of New Works. Those shows then are remounted in March at another professional theatre, usually the Bob Moss Theatre in Manhattan, but sometimes at venues like the Kennedy Center in Washington D.C.

We end with a week of finishing up our course work, public presentations of final projects, individual debriefings with each student and making plans for next summer.

As you move through successive summers, a wide array of courses are offered, and all have been designed to assist you in meeting your professional goals and expanding your artistic range. Classes like Writing Plays with Music, Writing for Young Audiences, Company Creation and Management, Dramaturgy, First Drafts, Docudrama, and, of course, Adaptation, taught last summer by Megan Gogerty.

I'm fond of saying that nothing is more dangerous than an overextended metaphor, but our program is a bit like that island—each summer is an episode jam-packed with learning, doing and sharing. If I am, in fact, this island's Professor, then Megan Gogerty has to be our Maryann. She is an Iowan full of good sense, enthusiasm and empathy. She is honest to a fault and leads by example. Each summer Megan shares her own work with our students with performances and readings of plays still in their earliest stages. She embodies what it is like to create an academic environment where faculty and students are all colleagues who just happen to have varying levels of experience.

Without extending the metaphor too far, maybe what Megan and Sean and the playwrights have created in this collection is a note in a bottle tossed out into the sea of new work, in the hope that someone else will find out about our little island and what we're doing here.

Please enjoy their note—and come visit us. You're sure to get a smile!

Todd Ristau
Program Director, Playwright's Lab at Hollins University

# THE ISLAND

A one-act play

By Sean Abley

## PLAYWRIGHT'S BIO

SEAN ABLEY is an award-winning playwright, screenwriter and journalist. He has over thirty plays published by Playscripts, Brooklyn Publishers, Heuer Publishing, Next Stage Press, and Eldridge Plays and Musicals, with titles like *End of the World (With Prom to Follow), The Adventures of Rose Red (Snow White's Less-Famous Sister), Horror High: The Musical* and *Attack of the Killer B's*. His television writing includes multiple episodes of *So Weird* (Disney Channel), *Sabrina, the Animated Series* (Disney/UPN), *Digimon* (Fox Family), as well as several pilots including *Bench Pressly, The World's Strongest Private Dick* with Ahmet Zappa, starring Bruce Campbell. His produced screenplays include the B-movies *Socket, Witchcraft 15: Blood Rose* and *Witchcraft 16: Hollywood Coven*. He was one on the founders of Chicago's prolific Factory Theater in 1992 (still going strong as of this writing), and the creator of the "Gay of the Dead" blog on Fangoria.com.

## SYNOPSIS

*The island is everything...*

Two members of a tourist group stranded on a deserted island take drastic action to be part of the action. But once they're full-fledged members of the group, their actions cause a catastrophic reaction.

## CHARACTERS

**THE SKIPPER** (m)

40s-60s. The boisterous captain of a small tourist boat.

**THE FIRST MATE** (m)

20s. The affable first mate of a small tourist boat.

**PROFESSOR** (m)

30s-40s. Handsome gentleman, thick head of hair, nice square jaw. A nonthreatening looking man who is completely threatening. First appears in disguise as TUGBOAT CAPTAIN and HELICOPTER PILOT.

**FARM GIRL** (f)

20s. Sweet and wholesome. First appears in disguise as LADY AIRPLANE PILOT, LADY SUBMARINE CAPTAIN and LADY TRAIN CONDUCTOR.

**NIELSEN** (m/f)

Any age. Official looking chap or lady in a crisp suit.

**TUGBOAT CAPTAIN** (m)

Played by actor playing PROFESSOR in disguise.

**HELICOPTER PILOT** (m)

Played by actor playing PROFESSOR in disguise.

| | |
|---|---|
| **LADY AIRPLANE PILOT** (f) | Played by actor playing FARM GIRL in disguise. |
| **LADY SUBMARINE CAPTAIN** (f) | Played by actor playing FARM GIRL in disguise. |
| **LADY TRAIN CONDUCTOR** (f) | Played by actor playing FARM GIRL in disguise. |
| **JET PILOT** (m/f) | A jet pilot. Change to LADY JET PILOT in dialogue if female. |
| **ASTRONAUT** (m/f) | Played by actor playing JET PILOT. Change to LADY ASTRONAUT in dialogue if female. |
| **SURFER** (m/f) | Played by actor playing JET PILOT. Change to LADY SURFER in dialogue if female. |

NOTE: The characters denoted as disguises for the PROFESSOR and FARM GIRL must be played by the character indicated, and may not be cast with separate actors in each role. The characters JET PILOT, ASTRONAUT and SURFER are listed together for doubling purposes, but may all be played by separate actors.

## <u>SETTING</u>

The beach of a deserted island out of time.

# THE ISLAND

## By Sean Abley

### Scene 1

(*THE ISLAND. ON THE BEACH. At LIGHTS UP, we hear SFX: studio audience laughter as if we've just walked in after the punchline to a joke. The SKIPPER, a boisterous man in his late 40s-50s, and the FIRST MATE, an affable goofball in his 20s, are celebrating with the LADY AIRPLANE PILOT. NOTE: All costumes should be shades of black, white and gray until further noted.*)

**FIRST MATE.** So you'll fly me, the skipper, the millionaire, his wife, the movie star, and some other people off the island?
**LADY AIRPLANE PILOT.** Of course! I'll just go fire up the Piper Cub and then we can leave this island behind forever!

(*LADY AIRPLANE PILOT exits.*)

**FIRST MATE.** You hear that, Skipper? We're rescued!
**SKIPPER.** I sure did, little pal!

(*SFX: A small propeller plane engine coming to life.*)

**FIRST MATE.** (*Calling off.*) Let's go everyone! We're rescued!

(*SFX: The small plane taking flight.*)

**SKIPPER.** She must be circling back to pick us all up.

(*SFX: The plane flying away. The sound of the engine fades out.*)

**SKIPPER.** Will you look at that?! She's flying away!
**FIRST MATE.** Hey! Lady Airplane Pilot! Come back!
**SKIPPER.** She flew away without even looking back.
**FIRST MATE.** Now we'll never get off the island.

**SKIPPER.** Next time, little pal. Let's go eat some of that coconut cream pie someone somehow figured out how to make without an oven.
**FIRST MATE.** Sounds good!

(*SFX: End credits sitcom theme as LIGHTS FADE TO BLACK.*)

### Scene 2

(*LIGHTS UP. On the beach. SFX: Audience laughter. SKIPPER and FIRST MATE are celebrating with TUGBOAT CAPTAIN.*)

**FIRST MATE.** You mean you can take me, the skipper, the millionaire, his wife, and some other random people off the island?
**TUGBOAT CAPTAIN.** Of course! I'll just go fire up my tugboat and then we can leave this island behind forever!

(*TUGBOAT CAPTAIN exits.*)

**FIRST MATE.** You hear that, Skipper? We're rescued!
**SKIPPER.** I sure did, little pal!

(*SFX: A tugboat engine coming to life.*)

**FIRST MATE.** (*Calling off.*) Let's go everyone! We're rescued!

(*SFX: The tugboat pulling away.*)

**SKIPPER.** He must be circling back to pick us all up.

(*SFX: The tugboat leaving. The sound of the engine fades out.*)

**SKIPPER.** Will you look at that?! He's leaving!
**FIRST MATE.** Hey! Mr. Tugboat Captain! Come back!
**SKIPPER.** He steered away without even looking back.
**FIRST MATE.** Now we'll never get off the island.

**SKIPPER.** Next time, little pal. Let's go play some records on that record player someone figured out how to make without the ability to mold plastic.
**FIRST MATE.** Sounds good!

*(SFX: End credits sitcom theme as LIGHTS FADE TO BLACK.)*

### Scene 3

*(LIGHTS UP. The beach. SFX: audience laughter. The SKIPPER and FIRST MATE celebrating with a LADY SUBMARINE CAPTAIN.)*

**FIRST MATE.** You mean you can take me, the skipper, the millionaire, his wife, and two other generic people off the island?
**LADY SUBMARINE CAPTAIN.** Of course! I'll just go fire up my submarine and then we can leave this island behind forever!

*(LADY SUBMARINE CAPTAIN exits.)*

**FIRST MATE.** You hear that, Skipper? We're rescued!
**SKIPPER.** I sure did, little pal!

*(SFX: A submarine engine coming to life.)*

**FIRST MATE.** *(Calling off.)* Let's go everyone! We're rescued!

*(SFX: The submarine moving away.)*

**SKIPPER.** She must be circling back to pick us all up.

*(SFX: The submarine motoring away. The sound of the engine fades out.)*

**SKIPPER.** Will you look at that?! She's leaving!
**FIRST MATE.** Hey! Lady Submarine Captain! Come back!
**SKIPPER.** She drove that submarine away without even looking back.
**FIRST MATE.** Now we'll never get off this island.

**SKIPPER.** Next time, little pal. Let's go wash our clothes in a washing machine someone somehow figured out how to make despite there being no electricity or soap on the island.

**FIRST MATE.** Sounds good!

(*SFX: End credits sitcom theme as LIGHTS FADE TO BLACK.*)


### Scene 4


(*LIGHTS UP. The beach. SFX: audience laughter. SKIPPER and FIRST MATE celebrate with HELICOPTER PILOT.*)

**FIRST MATE.** So you'll fly me, the skipper, the millionaire, his wife, the movie star, and a handful of people too uninteresting to name off the island?

**HELICOPTER PILOT.** Of course! I'll just go fire up the helicopter and then we can leave this island behind forever!

**FIRST MATE.** You hear that Skipper? We're rescued!

**SKIPPER.** Sure did, little pal!

(*HELICOPTER PILOT moves to leave, but reconsiders.*)

**HELICOPTER PILOT.** I have an idea. Why don't you come along with me to the helicopter?

**FIRST MATE.** What?

**HELICOPTER PILOT.** Why don't you come and get into the helicopter?

**FIRST MATE.** But...

**SKIPPER.** But next time! Let's go make waffles on a waffle iron even though we don't have flour for waffles or metal to make a waffle iron.

**HELICOPTER PILOT.** Listen to me. You can come with me. You can. And then we can go get your friends, and we can leave this island behind forever.

(*LADY TRAIN CONDUCTOR enters.*)

**LADY TRAIN CONDUCTOR.** What are you doing?

**HELICOPTER PILOT.** I've had enough.

**FIRST MATE.** So you'll... uh... train me, the skipper, the millionaire, his wife, the movie star, and an indeterminate number of other people off the island?

**LADY TRAIN CONDUCTOR.** You're going to ruin this!

**FIRST MATE.** You hear that, Skipper? We're rescued!

**SKIPPER.** I sure did, little pal!

(*Despite the fact no one has left the stage, SFX: A train engine coming to life.*)

**HELICOPTER PILOT.** We've done our part. We've stranded them on this island how many times? A dozen? Hundreds? We made a deal, and it's time for them to honor the agreement.

**FIRST MATE.** (*Calling off.*) Let's go everyone! We're rescued!

(*SFX: The train chugging out of the station.*)

**LADY TRAIN CONDUCTOR.** I just think we should wait for a signal from them.

**SKIPPER.** She must be circling back to pick us all up.

**HELICOPTER PILOT.** I'm not waiting any more. It's time for us to be.

(*SFX: The train fading away in the distance.*)

**SKIPPER.** Will you look at that?! She's taking the train away!

**FIRST MATE.** Hey! Lady Train Conductor! Come back!

**LADY TRAIN CONDUCTOR.** We have to get out of here! We can discuss this with them during the transition.

**SKIPPER.** She conducted that train away without even looking back.

**HELICOPTER PILOT.** There's never time.

**FIRST MATE.** Now we'll never get off the island.

**HELICOPTER PILOT.** I'm making time.

**SKIPPER.** Next time, little pal. Let's go make explosives out of coconuts and that gunpowder that mysteriously floated to the island in a wooden box!

**FIRST MATE.** Sounds good!

(*SFX: End credits sitcom theme as LIGHTS FADE TO BLACK, but this time we hear HELICOPTER PILOT and LADY TRAIN CONDUCTOR in the dark.*)

**LADY TRAIN CONDUCTOR.** We have to switch out. Come on!
**HELICOPTER PILOT.** I'm not moving.

### Scene 5

(*LIGHTS UP. The beach. SFX: audience laughter, but louder this time, as if it's a signal to the characters on the beach. SKIPPER, FIRST MATE, HELICOPTER PILOT and LADY TRAIN CONDUCTOR still in place.*)

**FIRST MATE.** So you'll take me, the skipper, the millionaire, his wife, the movie star, and some other people off the island?

(*HELICOPTER PILOT grabs FIRST MATE.*)

**HELICOPTER PILOT.** You're coming with me.
**FIRST MATE.** What are you doing?
**LADY TRAIN CONDUCTOR.** Let go of him!
**SKIPPER.** I sure did, little pal...
**FIRST MATE.** What's happening?!
**HELICOPTER PILOT.** You're coming with me and we're getting on that helicopter, or train.
**LADY TRAIN CONDUCTOR.** But we're supposed to strand them here!

(*SFX: ending credits theme. LIGHTS FADE TO BLACK as we hear FIRST MATE, SKIPPER, HELICOPTER PILOT and LADY TRAIN CONDUCTOR in the dark.*)

**SKIPPER.** Whoa, wait, next time little pal let's go play electric guitars made out of palm fronds—
**FIRST MATE.** (*Panicked.*) Sounds good!
**HELICOPTER PILOT.** No, you're coming with us. Stop struggling!

(*LIGHTS UP. The beach. SFX: audience laughter, but distorted, like someone's used a match on the audio tape. FIRST MATE, SKIPPER, HELICOPTER PILOT and LADY TRAIN CONDUCTOR still in place.*)

**LADY TRAIN CONDUCTOR.** Oh, God...
**HELICOPTER PILOT.** Don't say it!
**FIRST MATE.** (*Tries to get it out quickly.*) Soyou'llflymethe-skipperthemillionaire—

(*HELICOPTER PILOT claps his hands over FIRST MATE's mouth, preventing him from finishing his line. SFX: audience laughter, revved up, angry, a response to HELICOPTER PILOT's transgression.*)

**SKIPPER.** (*Panicked.*) I sure did, little pal!
**HELICOPTER PILOT.** (*RE: SKIPPER.*) Stop him!
**LADY TRAIN CONDUCTOR.** No!

(*FIRST MATE frees himself from HELICOPTER PILOT's grasp.*)

**FIRST MATE.** STOP IT!

(*FIRST MATE and SKIPPER back away from HELICOPTER PILOT and LADY TRAIN CONDUCTOR.*)

**FIRST MATE.** Stay back! Who are you? Why are you forcing us to leave the island when all we want to do is get off the island?

(*HELICOPTER PILOT removes his costume to reveal he is actually a PROFESSOR, a nice looking man, full head of hair, button down shirt with sleeves rolled up. Nonthreatening looking man who is completely threatening. The audience should recognize he also played the TUGBOAT CAPTAIN.*)

**FIRST MATE.** You!
**PROFESSOR.** Yes! Say who I am! Say it!
**FIRST MATE.** You're you. You. You know, one of the other people here on the island.
**PROFESSOR.** You can't say it, can you? (*To SKIPPER.*) What about you?

**SKIPPER.** Like my little pal said, you're one of the other people on the island.

**PROFESSOR.** And her?

(*LADY TRAIN CONDUCTOR doffs her costume to reveal she is the FARM GIRL, a sweet, wholesome young lady in her 20s who is quite angry at the moment. The audience should recognize she also played both LADY AIRPLANE PILOT and LADY SUBMARINE CAPTAIN.*)

**SKIPPER.** Well, she's some of the people on the island.

**PROFESSOR.** I told you.

**FARM GIRL.** You honestly don't know who I am?

**FIRST MATE.** Well, I know I have a bit of a crush on you.

(*FIRST MATE moves in for a very chaste kiss, but FARM GIRL holds him at bay.*)

**FARM GIRL.** I bake you coconut pie every week!

**PROFESSOR.** I built a radio from parts of your ship, and a washing machine, and an oven! You would starve to death if we weren't here, and you don't know who we are.

**FIRST MATE.** That's silly. You're the rest of the people on the island.

**PROFESSOR.** That's not enough! (*To an unseen entity.*) That's not enough!

**FIRST MATE.** I really don't understand what you're getting at. Why do you keep pretending to be other people and leaving us on the island?

**FARM GIRL.** We don't leave you here. We circle around to the other side and rejoin the group. We're here all the time!

**FIRST MATE.** Why? That makes no sense.

**PROFESSOR.** To keep you active, moving around. So you don't just sit there and do nothing. To keep you interesting.

**SKIPPER.** Interesting to who?

**PROFESSOR.** I have no idea. (*RE: unseen entity.*) They made a deal with us. Keep you interesting, and in exchange they'd give us something. They'd make us something. Because we're worth something. We all are.

**SKIPPER.** Make you what?

**FARM GIRL.** One of you!

**PROFESSOR.** One day I woke up and realized I had a choice. I could do what I want.

**FARM GIRL.** Me, too!

**PROFESSOR.** And on that day, they came to us and gave us the choice to help them. And I said I wanted something in return.

**SKIPPER.** You're already one of us. We see you every day.

**FARM GIRL.** But we want to be something more.

**PROFESSOR.** Someone worthy of knowing.

**FARM GIRL.** People who are here, on the island, that other people know.

**PROFESSOR.** An existence.

**FIRST MATE.** What does that mean?

**PROFESSOR.** That we exist. We live. We're here.

**SKIPPER.** Of course you do! We all do.

**PROFESSOR.** But now we're going to be part of this island.

**FARM GIRL.** We're going to matter.

**PROFESSOR.** (*To an unseen entity.*) We did what you asked!

**FIRST MATE.** Who are you talking to?

**PROFESSOR.** The Nielsen.

**FIRST MATE.** Who are the Nielsen?

**PROFESSOR.** They're the ones keeping you on the island.

(*SFX: End credits theme music that starts upbeat then grinds to a halt. LIGHTS FADE TO BLACK. We can hear PROFESSOR and FARM GIRL in the dark.*)

**PROFESSOR.** This is it!

**FARM GIRL.** I'm scared! Will it hurt?

**PROFESSOR.** No, can't you feel it? It's happening already!

**FARM GIRL.** I do! I feel it! Like I'm... real!

## Scene 6

(*LIGHTS UP. The beach in beautiful color. From this moment on all costumes and set pieces are brightly colored. SFX: audience laughter, brighter, more present than previous versions. FIRST MATE, SKIPPER, PROFESSOR and FARM GIRL are celebrating with a JET PILOT.*)

**FIRST MATE.** So you'll fly me, the skipper, the millionaire, his wife, the movie star, the professor and Mary Ann off the island?

**JET PILOT.** Of course! I'll just go fire up the jet and then we can leave this island behind forever!

(*JET PILOT exits.*)

**FIRST MATE.** You hear that, Skipper, Professor, Mary Ann? We're rescued!

**SKIPPER.** I sure did, little pal!

**FARM GIRL.** I'm Mary Ann...

(*SFX: A jet engine coming to life.*)

**FIRST MATE.** (*Calling off.*) Let's go everyone! We're rescued!

(*SFX: The jet taking flight.*)

**SKIPPER.** He must be circling back to pick us all up.

(*SFX: The jet flying away. The sound of the engine fades out.*)

**SKIPPER.** Will you look at that?! He's flying away!

**FIRST MATE.** Hey! Mr. Jet Pilot! Come back!

**SKIPPER.** He flew away without even looking back.

**FIRST MATE.** Now we'll never get off the island.

**SKIPPER.** Next time, little pal. Let's go write our memoirs on the typewriter the professor built for us out of pieces of the ship.

**FIRST MATE.** Sounds good!

**PROFESSOR.** Wait a minute!

**FIRST MATE.** What?

**PROFESSOR.** That's it?

**FIRST MATE.** What do you mean?

**PROFESSOR.** That's all we have to do? Just stand here and watch you two deal with jet pilots?

**FIRST MATE.** Well...

**PROFESSOR.** That's not enough.

**FIRST MATE.** What are you talking about?

**PROFESSOR.** I'm talking—

**FARM GIRL.** (*Interrupting.*) I want more. I want more than a name. I want a place. I want important things to do. I want something to go with my name.

**PROFESSOR.** Whoa, wait a minute. You got a name. That should be enough for you.

**FARM GIRL.** It should?

**PROFESSOR.** Of course it should. Did you have a name before?

**FARM GIRL.** No.

**PROFESSOR.** And now you do. You're welcome. Now let me handle the rest of this.

**FARM GIRL.** But I want more....

(*SFX: End credits sitcom theme as LIGHTS FADE TO BLACK.*)

**FARM GIRL.** I have a name and I want more!

### Scene 7

(*LIGHTS UP. The beach. SFX: audience laughter. FIRST MATE, SKIPPER, PROFESSOR and FARM GIRL celebrate with an ASTRONAUT. PROFESSOR tries to get into the action as the scene plays out.*)

**FIRST MATE.** So you'll take me, the skipper, the millionaire, his wife, the movie star, the professor and Mary Ann off the island?

**PROFESSOR.** That would—

**ASTRONAUT.** Of course! I'll just go fire up the rocket and then we can leave this island behind forever!

(*ASTRONAUT exits.*)

**FIRST MATE.** You hear that, Skipper? We're rescued!

**SKIPPER.** I sure did, little pal!

(*SFX: A rocket engine coming to life.*)

**PROFESSOR.** Let's all—

**FIRST MATE.** (*Calling off.*) Let's go everyone! We're rescued!

*(SFX: The rocket taking off.)*

**SKIPPER.** He must be circling back to pick us all up.

*(SFX: The rocket flying away. The sound of the engine fades out.)*

**SKIPPER.** Will you look at that?! He's flying away!
**PROFESSOR.** We could—
**FIRST MATE.** Hey! Mr. Astronaut! Come back!
**SKIPPER.** He steered away without even looking back.
**FIRST MATE.** Now we'll never get off the island.
**PROFESSOR.** How about we—
**FARM GIRL.** We could build something! We could build a boat!
**PROFESSOR.** Stop it!
**FIRST MATE.** Sounds good!
**PROFESSOR.** No, it doesn't sound good!
**FARM GIRL.** I contributed something! I came up with a plan! Wow, that feels great!
**PROFESSOR.** Would you just shut up! You don't have a plan. You have an idea. I have a plan. *(To FIRST MATE and SKIPPER.)* I'm not going to just stand here and watch the action. What good is being if you aren't doing?
**FIRST MATE.** *(To SKIPPER.)* They got what they want, but they're so unhappy. I don't understand.
**SKIPPER.** Next time, little pal. Let's go ride that bike around the professor built for us even though we have no rubber for the tires.

*(SFX: End titles theme music. LIGHTS FADE TO BLACK.)*

**PROFESSOR.** I'm not going to stand around and just support protons, neutrons and electrons! I want to contribute!

## Scene 8

(*LIGHTS UP. The beach. SFX: audience laughter. FIRST MATE, SKIPPER, PROFESSOR and MARY ANN celebrate with SURFER.*)

**FIRST MATE.** So you'll surf me, the skipper, the millionaire, his wife, the movie star, the professor and Mary Ann off the island?
**SURFER.** Of course! I'll just go snag a wave and then we can leave this island behind forever!

(*PROFESSOR pulls out a homemade gun and points it at the SURFER. EVERYONE freaks out.*)

**PROFESSOR.** I don't think so, Big Typhoonah!
**FARM GIRL.** Professor! Where did you get that gun?
**PROFESSOR.** I made it out of a coconut and metal I smelted from ore deposits in the cave across the island by using a tin cup from the ship.

(*SURFER moves over with FIRST MATE, SKIPPER and FARM GIRL.*)

**SKIPPER.** (*"Please put down the gun."*) Next time, little pal. Let's go—
**PROFESSOR.** Shut up!
**SURFER.** Are you going to shoot me?
**PROFESSOR.** I just might. (*To unknown entity.*) Hear that?! I just might! I just might shoot one of him!

(*NIELSEN's voice comes from nowhere and everywhere.*)

**NIELSEN.** (*Off.*) Go ahead.

(*ALL react.*)

**PROFESSOR / SURFER.** What?!
**NIELSEN.** (*Off.*) Feel free. Shoot him. We have thousands, millions more just like him.
**PROFESSOR.** You can't be serious.
**NIELSEN.** (*Off.*) Of course I am.

**PROFESSOR.** I will!

**SURFER.** Please, don't!

**FARM GIRL.** Professor, let's think this through—

**PROFESSOR.** I exist! I can do whatever I want! I can make choices!

**NIELSEN.** (*Off.*) That's true. You've been given that gift. You worked hard for it. So, do with it what you will.

**FARM GIRL.** Professor, don't!

**PROFESSOR.** I can! I will! I exist!

**SURFER.** Don't!

(*PROFESSOR aims for the SURFER, but accidentally shoots FIRST MATE instead. LIGHTS INSTANTLY SHIFT from sitcom happiness to harsh TV studio set warehouse lighting. EVERYONE panics. SKIPPER cradles the dying FIRST MATE as he dies.*)

**ALL.** (*Improvised panic.*)

**FIRST MATE.** (*Dying.*) You hear that, Skipper? We're rescued...

**SKIPPER.** I sure did, little pal...

**FIRST MATE.** Let's go everyone... We're rescued... (*Dies.*)

**FARM GIRL.** What have you done?!

**PROFESSOR.** What does it matter?

**FARM GIRL.** It matters!

**PROFESSOR.** To who?

**FARM GIRL.** To us! To the millionaire and his wife and the movie star! I agreed to your plan because it meant I could be. I thought that's what you wanted, too.

**PROFESSOR.** I did. I do! And now we can exist. We can be part of the island. We're here, now, among them and they know who we are. We can do what we want!

**FARM GIRL.** I wanted to build a boat and get off the island. That's what I wanted. Why couldn't we do that?

**PROFESSOR.** Because that's not my plan.

**FARM GIRL.** So?

**PROFESSOR.** I'm built for this. I make the plan. You're here to support my plan.

**FARM GIRL.** That's not fair! Why don't I get to do what you do? The Nielson guaranteed us both the same thing.

**PROFESSOR.** There are different levels of being.

**FARM GIRL.** How—

**PROFESSOR.** Don't ask me how I know that, I just do. Mary Ann, please. I didn't bring you along on my plan to have to battle with you. Don't make me use this coconut gun on you, too.

**FARM GIRL.** That's your plan? Murder is wrong! And don't ask me how I know that, I just do.

**PROFESSOR.** Is it?

**FARM GIRL.** How can you even question that?

**PROFESSOR.** He said they have millions more!

(*NIELSEN enters, an official looking chap or lady in a sharp suit.*)

**NIELSEN.** And that we do... of the worker bees, the tugboat captains and the like. Plenty of those.

**PROFESSOR.** See?

**NIELSEN.** (*To SURFER.*) You can go.

**SURFER.** Thank God!

(*SURFER exits.*)

**NIELSEN.** But what we don't have an endless supply of are these.

(*NIELSEN points to SKIPPER and FIRST MATE's dead body.*)

**PROFESSOR.** What's the difference?

**NIELSEN.** Those— (*Pointing off toward where all the guest stars exited.*) are just the accoutrements. You can change those out, throw them away, nothing really changes. These— (*Pointing to SKIPPER and FIRST MATE's dead body.*) are the heart and soul. You get rid of these, and the whole shebang dies.

**FARM GIRL.** And what happens when the shebang dies?

**NIELSEN.** Everything else comes to an end.

**FARM GIRL.** Everything?

**NIELSEN.** I'm afraid so.

**FARM GIRL.** Can't we just leave the island?

**NIELSEN.** I'm sorry dear, there is no off the island for you. You're here, on the island. That's it. If you're off the island, you're off here. There is no other here.

**FARM GIRL.** But... I know there is. I remember being on a farm...

**NIELSEN.** Yes, that was an idea. But you were never there. You were always here. Now, make no mistake, there are other heres. We have hundreds of heres percolating all the time. Each of them is an experiment.

**SKIPPER.** Can you slow down on that? I'm an old sea dog, my thinking isn't the best.

**NIELSEN.** You'll have to trust me when I tell you it doesn't matter. To you anyway. So the question is—What elements can we place in a here to best facilitate a nice, long life? A first mate, a skipper, a farm girl. Weather. Location. Emotions. For this here, we chose an island, a specific social caste system, identity issues, and after a bit, free will and the opportunity to define oneself. Not for everyone, obviously. We chose the two of you. And as you can see, unfortunately that didn't lead to a very long life for this here. (*Off FARM GIRL's reaction.*) I'm sorry, dear. I really was rooting for you. If it's any solace, we had no idea you'd be so intelligent. Our mistake, but you're paying for it and for that I apologize.

**FARM GIRL.** (*To PROFESSOR.*) You idiot! You killed us!

**PROFESSOR.** If inventing a coconut gun and shooting the first mate is the cause of our demise, then so be it. I'm ready to go. I've become. I've had my defining moment. I'm a murdering professor.

**FARM GIRL.** But that's not me! I don't feel like I'm ready to go. Why is it all based on your actions? I didn't do anything!

**NIELSEN.** But you did! You acted! You took control and made yourself. You did the most you could do.

**FARM GIRL.** I did?

**NIELSEN.** You inspired a name. "Mary Ann." Who else has a name? Everyone else is their job. Whatever it was that you became, it inspired "Mary Ann."

**FARM GIRL.** That doesn't seem like very much.

**NIELSEN.** (*Laughs.*) Yes, all you did was live. Just for a moment, you lived. Existed. Does that really feel so small for you?

**FARM GIRL.** I... you gave me the capacity for wanting more than I can have. Now it all feels... incomplete.

**NIELSEN.** We call those aspirations, which are best kept unrealized. It's better for dramatic tension.

**FARM GIRL.** I have to feel like this forever?

**NIELSEN.** No, just a few more moments. Then it will all be over. You won't exist so you won't have existed so you won't have any memory of what it feels like to be you right now. So enjoy the desire and anger and sadness and all those other emotions. They're all you've got.

**FARM GIRL.** You're a monster!

(*FARM GIRL exits.*)

**PROFESSOR.** Are we being punished? I can't tell if this is punitive or not.

**NIELSEN.** Oh, no. Not punished. It's just over. If anyone should be punished, it should be us for letting you build that gun. But then again, that's a mark of a successful here—thwarted expectations. It was definitely interesting. But perhaps a step too far. (*Points to SKIPPER.*) If you'd shot him, we might've been able to continue. But sadly, it was the first mate's island. I don't think even he knew that. But without him...

**PROFESSOR.** Understood.

(*NIELSEN moves to exit, then stops.*)

**NIELSEN.** A question. Was it worth it?

**PROFESSOR.** I don't know. Will I ever?

**NIELSEN.** You'll have a few moments to wrap everything up, but we'll be moving on very soon. (*To SKIPPER.*) Here, I'll give this to you. Enjoy it for a bit.

(*NIELSEN gestures at SKIPPER. SKIPPER is now cognizant of their situation.*)

**SKIPPER.** You were careless.

**PROFESSOR.** With the gun?

**SKIPPER.** (*Points to NIELSEN.*) No, him. My God, I feel terrible.

**NIELSEN.** You're welcome.

**SKIPPER.** And now what? We're going to die on this island?

**NIELSEN.** You're not going to die. You're just not going to be. It's painless, really.

(*NIELSEN exits.*)

**PROFESSOR.** Do you forgive me?

**SKIPPER.** I could. But I don't want to. I guess that was his gift. Goodbye, little pal.

(*SKIPPER exits, leaving FIRST MATE's dead body on stage.*)

**PROFESSOR.** (*A moment.*) I *have* been careless. With the gun and now I know carelessness. And anger and guilt. And joy. Pure joy. To exist is to be cursed with everything. Will I know everything after? I don't care. I know everything know. And it feels—

(*BLACKOUT.*)

## END OF PLAY

# GILLIAN'S ISLE

A ten-minute play

By Liesl Ehmke

## PLAYWRIGHT'S BIO

LIESL "LEE" EHMKE has a BA in Theatre from Principia College and is an MFA candidate in the Playwright's Lab at Hollins University. She is an educator, actor, director, and playwright. Liesl has had a number of ten-minute plays produced across the country, including *Internal Clock*, produced for the Sundown Collaborative Theatre's Shorts Works Festival in Denton, Texas (August 2015), *Gone with the Date*, produced for The Red Eye 10s Play Festival in Virginia, Kentucky, Colorado, Montana, California, and Germany (September 2015), *Break Up Alley*, produced by TRASH: A Theatre LILA Invention in Madison, WI (October 2015 and April 2015), and *Finding Nina*, commissioned by The Tesseract Theatre Company (St. Louis, MO) as part of an anthologized play, *A Mourning Hollow*, produced and published in October 2015. Her ten-minute play, *Behind My Smile*, was published in Tesseract Theatre Company's *2015 Curtain Openers: Six 10-minute Plays* (Polychoron Press).

## SYNOPSIS

*P.S. I love your money.*

Edgar plans a romantic getaway on a deserted island with his new wife, Gillian, but unbeknownst to him, Gillian has plans of her own. Will she get what she wants, or will she get a surprise of her own?

## CHARACTERS

**EDGAR** (m)

Adult male, married to GILLIAN, famous physicist and winner of the Nobel Prize.

**GILLIAN** (f)

Adult female, married to EDGAR.

**ANNE** (f)

Adult female, EDGAR and GILLIAN's servant.

## SETTING

A yacht.

# GILLIAN'S ISLE

## By Liesl Ehmke

(*LIGHTS UP.*

*GILLIAN sits in a lounge chair on the deck of a yacht. She is wearing a white robe with two slices of cucumber covering her eyes, and her hair wrapped in a white towel. EDGAR stands looking out at the open sea. He is wearing glasses, a tuxedo, and a straw hat, with sunscreen covering his nose. ANNE, dressed in a servant's uniform, stands to the side.*)

**EDGAR.** Gillian, my love, you have made me the happiest man in the world. I remember the attraction I felt the first moment I saw you. You were the nucleus to my electron. And in just two short weeks my affection for you has grown like a supernova five hundred times the size of our sun. When I proposed, I told you how much I loved you. How much, indeed. There is simply no human measurement in existence to quantify such a feeling. Love simply...is. I can't imagine there is anything that could ever change the way we feel about each other. Do you? (*Pause.*) Darling?

**GILLIAN.** How much longer? It smells horrendous.

**EDGAR.** It's the smell of the ocean, darling. It's refreshing.

**GILLIAN.** It's nauseating.

**EDGAR.** We could go back—

**GILLIAN.** NO! I mean...it's just a bit...chilly. That's all.

**EDGAR.** Perhaps if you put your wedding dress back on—

**GILLIAN.** I can't. It doesn't...fit anymore. The sea air must have shrunk it.

**EDGAR.** May I offer you my jacket instead? I seem to be getting a bit overheated as it were. This vest is rather heavy—

(*He starts to take off his tuxedo jacket, but ANNE interrupts.*)

**ANNE.** Excuse me, sir, but we're approaching land. It won't be long now. May I get either one of you a drink?

**GILLIAN.** (*To ANNE, but not directed to anywhere in particular.*) You. Whatever your name is. Come here.

**ANNE.** It's Anne.

**GILLIAN.** I wasn't asking. And I don't appreciate the barrage of questions.

**ANNE.** I asked you one question—

**GILLIAN.** The only two words I want to hear from you are "yes" and "ma'am." In that order.

**ANNE.** Yes, ma'am.

**GILLIAN.** When and if I want a drink, I'll let you know.

**ANNE.** Yes, ma'am.

**GILLIAN.** (*Pause.*) Long Island Ice Tea. Now.

**ANNE.** Yes, ma'am.

(*ANNE looks at EDGAR.*)

**EDGAR.** Nothing for me, thank you.

(*ANNE nods and crosses to a small bar.*)

**EDGAR.** I hope you like your gift, darling. I named it after you.

**GILLIAN.** A mound of silt surrounded by miles and miles of shark infested sea water. What's not to love?

**EDGAR.** Darling?

**GILLIAN.** It was a joke, Edgar. Stop pouting.

**EDGAR.** It's not that. I'm anxious about the weather. You were so insistent upon seeing the island tonight, but—

**GILLIAN.** (*Interrupting.*) Dear God, Edgar, let's not talk about the weather. It's so...common. Where's my Long Island Ice Tea?!

**ANNE.** Coming.

(*GILLIAN holds out her hand. ANNE places the drink in it.*)

**GILLIAN.** Aren't you forgetting something?

(*ANNE removes the two slices of cucumbers from GILLIAN's eyes. She stands in the back and takes a bite of one of the cucumber slices and chews it slowly glaring at GILLIAN unnoticed. GILLIAN takes a small sip. She makes a face.*)

**EDGAR.** What's wrong, darling?

**GILLIAN.** This is not a Long Island Ice Tea.

**EDGAR.** Are you sure?

**GILLIAN.** I'm not an idiot.

**EDGAR.** Sorry, darling. Anne, could you bring Mrs. Worthington, another Long Island Ice Tea?

**GILLIAN.** Not another Long Island Ice Tea. *A* Long Island Ice Tea. And be quick about it.

(*GILLIAN throws the glass overboard. ANNE crosses to the bar.*)

**EDGAR.** I don't think we're allowed to do that, darling. What seems to be troubling you? It's our honeymoon. We should be happy.

**GILLIAN.** Need I remind you what I've been through?

**EDGAR.** Been through, darling?

**GILLIAN.** All the media attention.

**EDGAR.** Oh, yes. That.

**GILLIAN.** Yes, that. I find it all so vexing. You and your "work." It's not as if no one has ever won the Nobel Prize before.

**EDGAR.** Still. It was an honor.

**GILLIAN.** I swear, Edgar, your ego is exhausting.

(*ANNE crosses over to GILLIAN with the drink. GILLIAN pulls out a tiny handgun and points it at EDGAR.*)

**GILLIAN.** Don't move. Either one of you.

**EDGAR.** Gillian? What on earth are you doing?

**GILLIAN.** I no longer wish to be your wife.

**EDGAR.** But we exchanged wedding vows just this morning. You said you loved me.

**GILLIAN.** I said no such thing.

**EDGAR.** True. You never said the words, but it was certainly implied. Are you sure you're not just feeling anxious about...tonight?

**GILLIAN.** What on earth are you referring to?

**EDGAR.** Consummating our marriage, of course. But I can assure you, there's no need to worry. I've been reading up on the subject.

(*GILLIAN takes the Long Island Iced Tea from ANNE, drinks it all, and throws the empty glass overboard.*)

**GILLIAN.** I wouldn't have sex with you if you were the last man on this yacht.

**EDGAR.** Is this foreplay? I skipped that chapter.

**GILLIAN.** Jump.

**EDGAR.** You can't be serious?

**GILLIAN.** Jump.

**EDGAR.** Gillian. I love you.

**GILLIAN.** Edgar, don't grovel, it's so unattractive.

**EDGAR.** You have wounded me deeply. But your happiness means everything to me. If it's a divorce you want, you can have it.

**GILLIAN.** I want your money.

**EDGAR.** You're entitled to half.

**GILLIAN.** And yet I want it all.

**EDGAR.** You're a famous movie star. You don't need my money.

**GILLIAN.** But the IRS does. Something about tax evasion. It's all very tedious. (*To ANNE.*) Another Long Island Iced Tea.

(*ANNE doesn't respond. GILLIAN points the gun at her.*)

**GILLIAN.** I believe the words you're searching for are, "Yes, ma'am."

**ANNE.** I'm afraid I can't comply.

**GILLIAN.** No matter. I'll make my own celebratory Long Island Iced Tea after I leave the two of you treading water miles and miles from shore. Say hello to the sharks for me. Now jump.

**ANNE.** I'm taking you into custody for attempted murder.

**GILLIAN.** What are you talking about?

**ANNE.** I'm with the CIA. I've been assigned to protect your husband for reasons of national security.

**EDGAR.** What?

**GILLIAN.** Is this about that ridiculous prize he won for his work in astrology? I didn't know people were in that much need of having their horoscopes read. Pathetic.

**ANNE.** It was the Nobel Prize in Physics, you idiot. Astrophysics to be exact. What this man knows could save our planet from certain destruction. But it won't save you.

**EDGAR.** But—

**GILLIAN.** Shut up, Edgar!

**ANNE.** I find you most disagreeable. It will be a pleasure to see you locked away behind bars for a very, very long time.

**GILLIAN.** Sorry to disappoint you, my dear, but you've forgotten something very important.

**ANNE.** What's that?

**GILLIAN.** I have a gun and I'm not afraid to use it.

(*GILLIAN points the gun at ANNE and pulls the trigger.*)

**EDGAR.** No!

(*EDGAR jumps in front of ANNE protectively. EDGAR is shot. He falls. ANNE rushes to his side.*)

**ANNE.** You won't get away with this.

**GILLIAN.** Oh, but I already have. I have a very convincing story to tell the authorities. We were blown off course by a terrible storm. In all the commotion, the two of you fell overboard and were lost at sea.

**ANNE.** They won't believe your lies.

**GILLIAN.** Oh my dear, I've made a career out of lying. I'm very good at it. (*Suddenly breaks out into very convincing crocodile tears.*) My husband?! Gone?! No! No, it can't be! How will I live?! How will I go on?! (*Pause, breaking character.*) Did someone say "will"? (*Laughs wickedly.*)

**ANNE.** "You've only got one shot and it'll take more than that to stop me!"

**GILLIAN.** A line from the 2002 movie *The Count of Monte Cristo* delivered by Edmund Dantes just before his archenemy Fernand Mondego shoots. Only I won't miss.

(*GILLIAN points the gun at ANNE and pulls the trigger. ANNE is shot. She falls. GILLIAN tosses the gun overboard and smiles. She walks over to the bar and makes herself another Long Island Iced Tea. ANNE begins to move. She stands up and faces GILLIAN. GILLIAN is in shock.*)

**GILLIAN.** How?

(*ANNE reveals she is wearing a bulletproof vest.*)

**ANNE.** You're under arrest.

(*GILLIAN throws her glass of Long Island Iced Tea at ANNE, and screams in anger as she rushes towards her. ANNE braces herself.*

*GILLIAN slips on the tea and falls overboard and out of sight. ANNE rushes to the side of the boat.)*

**GILLIAN.** (*Off.*) Don't just stand there like an idiot. Help me!
**ANNE.** Take my hand.

(*ANNE leans over and reaches out her hand.*)

**GILLIAN.** (*Off.*) Oh dear God, hurry up! There's a shark!
**ANNE.** I've got you!

(*ANNE grabs GILLIAN's hand. There is a scream. When she pulls her up out of the water, it's just a bloody arm. ANNE looks over the side of the yacht and cringes. EDGAR begins to move. ANNE rushes over to help him up.*)

**EDGAR.** What happened?
**ANNE.** Gillian shot you.
**EDGAR.** She what?
**ANNE.** She shot you. If she had just waited a few minutes more, the sedative I gave her would have put her to sleep and she'd be alive.
**EDGAR.** What happened? Where is she?
**ANNE.** She attacked me and accidentally fell overboard. That's all that's left of her.

(*ANNE indicates the bloody arm.*)

**EDGAR.** Oh dear. That is tragic. (*Pause.*) But I don't understand. How am I not dead?
**ANNE.** I have a confession to make, Mr. Worthington, the vest I insisted you wear this morning isn't actually a new fashion design by Ralph Lauren. It's a bulletproof vest.
**EDGAR.** I don't know what to say. You saved my life.
**ANNE.** Actually, Mr. Worthington, you saved mine. You had no idea you were wearing that vest, and yet you took a bullet for me. No one's ever done that for me before.

(*The clap of thunder can be heard. A flash of lightning can be seen.*)

**ANNE.** There's a storm coming, Mr. Worthington. We must get back to port immediately.

**EDGAR.** Yes, of course. (*Pause.*) Anne.

**ANNE.** Yes?

**EDGAR.** Call me, Edgar.

(*She smiles. The yacht engine is turned on and begins to move away. LIGHTS OUT.*)

### END OF PLAY

# JUMP SHIP

**A ten-minute play**

**By Lydia Stewart**

## PLAYWRIGHT'S BIO

LYDIA STEWART is a playwright, director and teacher from Kingman, IN, and an MFA candidate in the Playwrights Lab at Hollins University. She has a Bachelor's degree in Creative Writing and an MA in Dramatic Production from Bob Jones University. She is a public school teacher and a free-lance theater director. Her most recent piece, *Chrysopylae*, was produced at Bob Jones University in April of 2016. *Whales Outside the Window* was produced there in 2015. She is a free-lance writer and has developed several children's programs for community and religious theater. Her most recent publication *After the Fire* was published by Bible Truth Music in 2016.

## SYNOPSIS

*If we prefer to live in ignorance, those who see clearly are in the most danger.*

Wilson is the only one concerned about the storm; the rest either ignore it or pretend that it doesn't exist. He can either choose to stay among the madness...or choose the one way out that will get their attention.

## CHARACTERS

**CAPTAIN** (m)          Sees the storm but prefers to use it for his own ends.

**WILSON** (m)          Has clear vision; he is the only one who sees the storm for what it is.

**GINGER** (f)          She might be able to see if she tried; there is hope.

**EUNICE** (f)          Can only see and think of herself.

**THURSTON** (m)          Can only see and think of himself.

## SETTING

A ship.

## PRODUCTION NOTES

An absurdist play. Sounds of a storm are important.

# JUMP SHIP

## By Lydia Stewart

### Scene 1

(*On deck of a small ship. An epic storm—loud and windy. The CAPTAIN is in a rain slicker, steering, braving the elements. WILSON is holding onto the mast. Three chairs are positioned around a table on the lower deck.*)

**CAPTAIN.** Fine day for a little boat ride, ain't it!

**WILSON.** My stomach objects!

**CAPTAIN.** You're lucky! First ride out and you get a storm! Just watch me navigate these waves!

**WILSON.** We've got to turn around!

**CAPTAIN.** Nothing doing! I love a good storm! We're headed straight for the eye of the hurricane!

**WILSON.** What?!

**CAPTAIN.** Gives me a thrill! And everyone loves 'em!

**WILSON.** You can't do that! We could DIE out here...

**CAPTAIN.** Don't be ridiculous! I'm the captain!

**WILSON.** So?!

**CAPTAIN.** The passengers hired me as their captain! So of course we'll be fine! My judgment is impeccable!

**WILSON.** And what do I tell the passengers about you driving us into a storm?

**CAPTAIN.** Nothing! Say it's a beautiful sunny day! That's what I promised them. They'll believe anything I say. They have to—they wanted to set sail!

**WILSON.** Is that how you've always captained a ship!?

**CAPTAIN.** And by how I feel after lunch! Speakin' of—it's about time to serve the passengers their free lunch! 'Sposin' you trot down to galley and serve up grub! And remember, follow the script I gave you—make it real nice!

(*WILSON lurches down to a door below deck.*)

**WILSON.** Ladies and gentleman! There is a colossal storm bearing down on us and the Captain is knowingly steering us straight into—

**CAPTAIN.** Wilson! Don't bother with trifles! Serve lunch!

**WILSON.** Aye, Captain. (*He reads a paper from his pocket.*) It is now time for Captain's lunch specialty: fresh tuna with homemade wasabi and seaweed... (*He gags.*) ...rice pilaf... (*He gags again.*) ...with a side of crab legs in butter... (*He throws up over the railing.*)

(*GINGER enters, looking fresh and happy. She seems oblivious to the storm.*)

**GINGER.** Two orders of crab legs, please! It's such a beautiful day— all this sunshine makes me hungry!

**WILSON.** Would you care for a side of mutiny with that?

**GINGER.** You're silly!

(*EUNICE and THURSTON enter behind her.*)

**EUNICE.** I agree, dear, I LOVE the sunshine, but salt air just isn't fit for me. It really isn't.

**THURSTON.** Me, I'm excited about that fresh tuna! We get out a bit further and I'll do some deep-sea fishing—then we'll have swordfish steaks! But right now—

(*They sit in the chairs on deck. They don't seem to notice the storm that blows their hair and hats.*)

**THURSTON.** Rice pilaf!

**WILSON.** Sunshine? Fishing?! Are you delusional? How about a nice appetizer of "take over the ship from the nut job of a Captain who is steering us toward certain doom?"

**CAPTAIN.** Get on with it, Wilson! This ship doesn't keep free lunches waiting!

**WILSON.** Ayesir!

(*He exits, gagging.*)

**GINGER.** I can work on my tan while we eat—this is the perfect spot!

**EUNICE.** I'll get a sunburn. I always have to wear these wide hats—
    my skin is so sensitive.
**THURSTON.** Just freckles, dear.
**EUNICE.** No, SENSITIVE skin. And its probably skin cancer.
**THURSTON.** Psht. Freckles.
**EUNICE.** Men. They don't understand. All they care about is food.
**THURSTON.** Probably true! More than one kind of food, though! (*He*
    *openly enjoys looking at Ginger.*)
**EUNICE.** Thirsty, don't be crude.
**THURSTON.** Eunice, don't be a prude.

(*GINGER giggles. WILSON returns with food. He fights the wind and
struggles to stay upright. He drops the tray of food, preferably upside
down. None of it falls off. It is clearly fake and glued to the trays. It
would fabulous if it bounced.*)

**WILSON.**  Darn it! I'm sorry!

(*He bounces it for good measure, trying to show them its fake.*)

**WILSON.** Oh no! Now you can't eat it!
**GINGER.** Five-second rule!
**EUNICE.** No harm done.
**THURSTON.** Just blow on it.
**WILSON.** Blow on it?
**THURSTON.** Blow on it, boy! Perfectly safe.
**GINGER.** I'm even more excited to eat crab legs that bounce!

(*WILSON sets the tray on the table.*)

**WILSON.** I'm pretty sure that wouldn't be good for you! Similarly,
    not stopping the Captain from taking us to the bottom of the ocean
    isn't healthy! Storm! A massive storm! Look around you! HE is
    driving us further into IT. If we don't DO SOMETHING—
**EUNICE.** Why are you shouting at us?
**WILSON.** THE STORM! I'M SHOUTING OVER THE—
**THURSTON.** Aren't you going to serve us?
**WILSON.** Urp...I...urp...

(*He runs to the railing to throw up.*)

**WILSON.** How can you possibly eat during...THIS!

(*They start to eat. Or at least they think they're eating.*)

**THURSTON.** Is this what you call a storm—sunny little swells like this?
**GINGER.** What kind of sailor are you?
**EUNICE.** Mmm...I love the pilaf!
**WILSON.** But you're not—that's not—Captain! Captain!

(*He staggers to the Captain.*)

**WILSON.** These people—the storm! They really—
**CAPTAIN.** Believe in me? Yep!
**WILSON.** They're completely senseless!
**CAPTAIN.** Yep! But they liked me! So I give them what they signed up for! I even advertise that I will take you into catastrophic storms—"make your life thrilling again"! for boat rides—so I deliver!
**WILSON.** They could be swept overboard!
**CAPTAIN.** Well, tell them to hang on!
**WILSON.** HANG ON, YOU IDIOTS!
**THURSTON.** Did he just call us—?
**EUNICE.** How rude!
**GINGER.** (*Giggling.*) He's funny!
**WILSON.** What's the matter with these people!
**CAPTAIN.** Get with the program. What's the matter with YOU?
**WILSON.** I needed a job! I didn't think—
**CAPTAIN.** And I need a sailor who keeps quiet and does what he's told!
**WILSON.** And what if I don't?!
**CAPTAIN.** Then jump overboard!
**WILSON.** And when I don't come back?
**CAPTAIN.** They won't miss you.
**GINGER.** Sailor-man! You should! You should go swimming!
**EUNICE.** It would be dreadful for my skin!
**THURSTON.** No one said you should.
**EUNICE.** I was just saying...
**GINGER.** Let's go swimming!

**EUNICE.** Don't be silly, dear—you can't swim for half an hour after eating.

**GINGER.** Oh, right.

**CAPTAIN.** Well? Go, or stay?

**WILSON.** Ginger—Ginger—look around you. Can you see these waves?! These clouds? This wind?? We're all going to be drowned if we don't turn this boat around!

**CAPTAIN.** Drown yourself early and give us a few moments peace!

**WILSON.** Don't you care?

**CAPTAIN.** Go or stay?

**GINGER.** He doesn't mean it, sailor-man! He's a funny captain!

**WILSON.** You two—rich idiots!

**THURSTON.** I beg your pardon—!

**WILSON.** YOU'RE GOING TO DROWN!

**THURSTON.** Don't be stupid. I can swim. I was in the Navy!

**WILSON.** They're oblivious!

**CAPTAIN.** GO OR STAY??

**WILSON.** I'll lose either way!

**GINGER.** It's just a swim! You're getting awfully excited over a swim, Sailor-man. Are you sure you're alright?

**WILSON.** You really can't—? Can't see—?

**GINGER.** There's no storm, silly. Blue skies for miles.

**WILSON.** Just a swim... Ginger...I'm either delusional, or you are. If it's really a beautiful sunny day...I'll just drop into the water and have myself a swim and then climb back in.

**GINGER.** Wait half an hour and I'll join you!

**WILSON.** But if I disappear...if I don't come back...then you need to believe that something is going on. That you're in danger. That you need to turn this boat around or die.

(*WILSON goes to the railing. The wind picks up, howling and blowing. He lifts himself up to the railing...*)

**WILSON.** Just a swim...

(*He drops over the edge.*)

**GINGER.** Have a nice swim!

**CAPTAIN.** Well, that's less complicated!

**THURSTON.** What's that?

**CAPTAIN.** I say, this is one great trip!

**THURSTON.** Best little voyage we've ever had! Think we can go fishing soon?

**CAPTAIN.** Almost there!

**EUNICE.** Oh huzzah!

**GINGER.** Sailor-man? Where did he go? Captain? Captain! Where did Sailor-man go? Won't we stop for him?

**CAPTAIN.** Oh, no—didn't you see the big sea turtle that he rode away on? He'll find another port. Another ship. One where he fits in. Forget him.

**EUNICE.** Already forgotten!

**THURSTON.** Who?

**GINGER.** But...but...we can't just...LEAVE him, Captain!

**CAPTAIN.** Excellent day for a voyage!

**GINGER.** Captain! Eunice? Thurston?

(*They ignore her.*)

**GINGER.** It's getting chilly out here all of a sudden...

(*She looks around as if she is just beginning to see.*

*LIGHTS FADE. Sounds of storm increase.*)

### **END OF PLAY**

# LILLI'S LOST AT SEA

**A ten-minute play**

**By Jessica Burton**

## PLAYWRIGHT'S BIO

JESSICA BURTON is from Vancouver in the rainy state of Washington, and is currently pursuing her Master of Fine Arts degree in the Playwright's Lab at Hollins University in Roanoke, VA. She received her undergraduate Bachelor of Arts Degree in May of 2015 from the University of Great Falls, in Great Falls, MT. Jessica is passionate about the performing arts, having been involved on and off stage from the age of three and loving every minute of it. Before returning to Hollins for her second summer, Jessica's piece, *Of Promises And Unsaid Goodbyes*, had a CenterPiece staged reading at the Waldron Stage in Downtown Roanoke, VA in May of 2016. Upon the start of her second summer, Jessica had a lab reading of her two-act play, *The Dream Weaver*, and participated as an actress in Ben Jolivet's play, *Cold*. Some of Jessica's favorite roles include Roxie Hart in *Chicago*, Marilyn Monroe in *The Dead Legend* at the New York Musical Theater Festival, Rosalie in *Decision Height*, as well as working on the choreography for *South Pacific*. Her background as a technician includes poster artwork design, lighting, sound, choreography, scenic detail painting and design, directing, and stage managing. Jessica is also pursuing her teaching certificate in dance while working for Dance Evolution Studio in Camas, WA as a teacher's assistant for the Evolution Preschool.

## SYNOPSIS

*They must find a way or remain lost at sea.*

What was supposed to be a three-hour tour turns into a group becoming lost at sea for three days. Now the group must come together if they are to find their way back home. Will this group make it back to land? Stay tuned.

## CHARACTERS

**LILLI** (f)

**AUNT BOBBY** (f)

**TOURIST** (m)

**TOURIST WIFE** (f)

**MODEL** (m)

**INVENTOR** (f)

**MARION** (m)

## SETTING

Setting takes place on the deck of a boat, but it does not have to be entirely decorated like a boat.

# LILLI'S LOST AT SEA

## By Jessica Burton

(*A pacific bluefin boat with a crow's nest gently rocks in the middle of the sea. Acting first mate, LILLI looks through her binoculars, searching for land.*)

**LILLI.** No sign of land yet. (*Looks at a map and gazes at the compass.*) We couldn't have gone out that far from land.

(*Acting Skipper, AUNT BOBBY enters.*)

**AUNT BOBBY.** How goes it my young first mate?

**LILLI.** Nothing so far. How's everyone holding up?

**AUNT BOBBY.** Terrible! I don't know how much longer I'll be able to distract them. The passengers won't last if we don't do something about our little...situation.

**LILLI.** What do you mean we? I've been up here, keeping watch and manning the ship, while you've been doing nothing.

**AUNT BOBBY.** That's not true! I've helped with steering the ship.

**LILLI.** Need I remind you, it's thanks to a certain someone we're stuck out in the middle of nowhere.

**AUNT BOBBY.** It's not that bad.

**LILLI.** Not that bad!? Who thought of doing this idiotic scheme and sold all of our food to the passengers?

**AUNT BOBBY.** I wanted to make a couple of extra bucks. Nothing wrong with that.

**LILLI.** You were supposed to ration the food! It's thanks to you, I have only half of a ham sandwich.

**AUNT BOBBY.** I couldn't help it, I was hungry! Come on...at least we're not ship wrecked on an island.

**LILLI.** Oh sure! That just makes our situation sound so much better, Aunt-

**AUNT BOBBY.** Shh! Don't call me that! Call me Skipper, remember?

**LILLI.** You've got to be kidding me?

**AUNT BOBBY.** What was that Lillian?

**LILLI.** I could have had a normal day at the beach, but no! I got pulled into a half-witted scheme by my con of an aunt.

**AUNT BOBBY.** Puts money in the bank sweetie.

**LILLI.** I can't believe this... at least I'm actually trying to find a way home.

(*LILLI holds the binoculars up once more while the TOURIST and TOURIST WIFE enter.*)

**TOURIST.** Excuse me lady Skipper, but just how much longer will the tour be lasting?

**AUNT BOBBY.** Uh...my first mate and I are working on that at the moment-

**LILLI.** Just me actually!

**AUNT BOBBY.** But we should be seeing land anytime time now.

**TOURIST WIFE.** Gosh, that storm we rode in was just a lovely detour on your part, but didn't you say that we would be back after a three-hour tour?

**AUNT BOBBY.** Oh...we're taking the scenic route back to the harbor!

**LILLI.** Apparently, the scenic route that takes 3 DAYS!

**AUNT BOBBY.** Oh, just feel that ocean breeze!

(*TOURIST and TOURIST WIFE make their way back inside the boat.*)

**TOURIST WIFE.** Gosh! These tours sure do everything. Don't they dear?

**TOURIST.** Just think, if we hadn't come on this tour, we would have gone to Universal Studios instead.

(*TOURIST and TOURIST WIFE exit.*)

**AUNT BOBBY.** Tourists these days. They'll buy into anything.

**LILLI.** Now that's just mean.

**AUNT BOBBY.** Don't you turn coy and innocent with me. You got a pretty good deal helping me on this.

**LILLI.** I don't know what you're talking about.

(*MARION enters.*)

**MARION.** What's shakin' Lill?

**LILLI.** Ah...um...hi.....Marion....

**MARION.** I haven't seen you down below in a while.

(*LILLI checks MARION out.*)

**LILLI.** What? Oh! I've been busy. So um...whatcha up to...?

**MARION.** I thought about hanging out here for a while. Would you mind if I joined you?

**LILLI.** That would be just love-

**AUNT BOBBY.** No time for that right now! We have something to work on...remember Lillian!

**LILLI.** Huh...I do?

**MARION.** Oh, gee, that's sad. Maybe we can hang out later when the tour's over.

**LILLI.** (*Talks as if she is in a trance.*) Yeah...that would be great...

**MARION.** But what can I do now? I know! I'll go hang out with that lovely Inventor. She seemed to be working on an interesting device. I'll catch you later, Lilli.

(*MARION exits. LILLI looks toward AUNT BOBBY.*)

**AUNT BOBBY.** Do not give me that look Lilli...um...look on the bright side!

**LILLI.** What's the bright side?

**AUNT BOBBY.** You may have a date with him if we ever get back to land. Also...what about those lovey-dovey looks you gave him?

**LILLI.** I...that does not prove anything!

(*MODEL enters.*)

**MODEL.** What's up everyone? Are we nearing port yet?

**LILLI.** Hummna...humma...nuh....hello....

**MODEL.** So what's the status?

**LILLI.** Uh....

**AUNT BOBBY.** We're working on it, kid. We're going all out on this tour just for you. Isn't that right, Lilli?

**LILLI.** Uh....uhh huh....

**MODEL.** Do you even know where you're going?

**AUNT BOBBY.** Of course! We haven't steered you wrong yet, have we?

**MODEL.** I suppose so—

**LILLI.** Umm...while we work on finding land, why don't you just...relax...hangout...and possibly...work on your tan...

**MODEL.** Pardon?

**LILLI.** I mean for your job! Didn't you tell me you're like a very famous super model? It's important to always keep a good tan for yourself, right?

**MODEL.** Hmm...I suppose you're right. I should work on my tan. I'm not going to get many opportunities for one when I get my next modeling gig.

(*MODEL lies on the deck below while LILLI slowly aims her binoculars watching him.*)

**LILLI.** Uhh huh....yes, yes, you should...

**AUNT BOBBY.** Lillian...get your head out of the gutter, why don't ya?

**LILLI.** I merely made a suggestion for him.

**AUNT BOBBY.** And you think I'm bad.

(*INVENTOR enters.*)

**INVENTOR.** Any sign of shore yet Skipper?

**AUNT BOBBY.** We should be there soon.

**INVENTOR.** Uh...huh...I find that hard to logically believe Skipper.

**AUNT BOBBY.** Oh, you do!...Do you?

**INVENTOR.** I believe we are lost at sea, are we not?

**AUNT BOBBY.** Absolutely not—!

**LILLI.** Oh would you just admit it already!

**AUNT BOBBY.** Lillian! Don't say that!

**LILLI.** Yes, it's true. That woman who you've called Skipper is a fraud. She's my aunt who loves to find ways to con people and gain money.

**INVENTOR.** I figured as much.

**LILLI.** Also, I had absolutely no part in this what so ever! I'm just her sweet, innocent, visiting niece who got pulled into something she did not want to be part of. I just wanted to enjoy a day at the beach. I am sorry to say we have no idea what we are doing...exactly.

**AUNT BOBBY.** Lillian! My sweet, little, first mate!

**LILLI.** You brought this on yourself and stop calling me, Lillian! My name is Lilli and I am not your first mate!

(*TOURIST and TOURIST WIFE enter.*)

**TOURIST.** What's going on? Have we reached land yet?
**TOURIST WIFE.** Ooh, maybe it's another surprise stop on the tour!

(*MARION enters.*)

**MARION.** What's happening?

(*MODEL stands up.*)

**MODEL.** Did I just hear that we're really lost at sea?
**LILLI.** Come on Skipper, tell them the truth.
**ALL EXCEPT AUNT BOBBY.** Is it true?!
**AUNT BOBBY.** Okay, okay you got me! It's true we're...lost at sea!

(*Group gasps!*)

**AUNT BOBBY.** And...I'm not...a real skipper!

(*Group gasps again!*)

**TOURIST.** Great Scott!
**TOURIST WIFE.**  Oh golly gee!
**MODEL.** That's a bummer!
**MARION.** How tragic.
**INVENTOR.** Truly unfortunate.
**AUNT BOBBY.** I know I've messed up folks and I'm truly sorry about all of this, but I have one thing to say...due to the nature and extension of our unfortunate circumstance there will absolutely be no refunds.

(*Group groans.*)

**LILLI.** So...anybody have any ideas of how we can possibly find our way back to society?
**INVENTOR.** Actually, yes. I have created just the invention that should be able to assist us.

(*Group cheers!*)

**LILLI.** What is this invention?

**INVENTOR.** You see, using the electrical power of two potatoes, a cell phone battery, two needles, tooth paste, fishing line, a magnet, a piece of gum, a boat antenna, and a piece of wood, I have created a telegraph device.

(*Group gasps!*)

**MARION.** That's amazing, Miss Inventor! So this is the device you were working on earlier.

**MODEL.** But isn't that like a really old device?

**INVENTOR.** Yes, but using the homemade telegraph, we can send an SOS message out in Morse code to call for help.

**TOURIST WIFE.** This really is some vacation, huh honey!

**TOURIST.** Just wait till we tell the kids back at home about this!

**LILLI.** So you can send out the message?

**INVENTOR.** Oh no. I'm an inventor! I can only invent devices. I don't know anything about the use of Morse code or its language.

**LILLI.** What kind of inventor comes up with an idea like that, but doesn't know how to use Morse code?

**INVENTOR.** An inventor who's too busy to learn such an ancient language.

**MODEL.** I don't think it's that ancient?

**LILLI.** No. Latin is an ancient language. Morse code is not!

**AUNT BOBBY.** There goes that idea.

**TOURIST.** Then what can we do? If we've been on a boat for three days when it was actually a three-hour tour, is there no hope for us?

**TOURIST WIFE.** How will we ever survive?

(*Group begins to panic.*)

**MODEL.** This is terrible! I have a gig in LA in a few days.

**AUNT BOBBY.** This is all my fault! Oh...curse my greed for money and my urge to con.

**INVENTOR.** It is a sad day indeed!

**LILLI.** Wait a second! I've got it, it's so simple!

**TOURIST.** What a cruel world this is!

**TOURIST WIFE.** I never even got to go to the Wonderful World of Harry Potter!

**LILLI.** Guys! Guess what?

**TOURIST.** Do you have any more ideas, Miss Inventor?

**INVENTOR.** At the moment, no.

**LILLI.** Hey! Instead of wondering about our impending doom, why don't we just use our cell phones!

**AUNT BOBBY.** Our cell phones?

**LILLI.** Yes! We can use the GPS systems on our phones! With any luck, if we're close enough to land, we can still get a signal on our phones. And...we have a signal!

(*Group cheers!*)

**LILLI.** And from the looks of it we are...10 miles away from land.

(*Group cheers again!*)

**MODEL.** Sweet! Now I can still make it to LA!

**INVENTOR.** How fortunate for us.

**TOURIST / TOURIST WIFE.** Our vacation has been saved!

**MARION.** We won't have to live off of raw fish and seaweed for the rest of our lives!

(*Group cheers again!*)

**AUNT BOBBY.** All right then, which way do we need to go?

**LILLI.** According to GPS, we need to head...uh oh...

**AUNT BOBBY.** What's wrong?

**LILLI.** My phone. It just...died.

(*Group gasps.*)

**LILLI.** Wait! What about everyone else?

**TOURIST.** Our phones stopped working after the first night.

**TOURIST WIFE.** You see! We took so many pictures, we ended up using all the battery on both of our phones.

**TOURIST.** Like the beautiful shots we got of the dolphins!

**TOURIST WIFE.** Or the orca pod!

**TOURIST.** Or the sea gulls!

**TOURIST WIFE.** Don't forget the lightning storm!

**TOURIST.** And those stunning shots of the whale shark that went under the boat! Remember that dear!

**TOURIST WIFE.** Oh yes that was just—

**LILLI.** It's okay! Let's not panic yet. Anyone else's phone working?!

**INVENTOR.** I used part of my phone to create the telegraph.

**MARION.** I...lost power while playing Candy Crush and Soda Crush.

**MODEL.** I think my phone still has battery power. (*Pulls out his phone and looks.*) Nope! It's off. Strange, I could have swore I had...oh that's right! I talked with my agent for a couple hours the other day. I had to hear what my schedule was when we got back.

**MARION.** You had signal on your phone all this time and you didn't think to tell anyone?

**MODEL.** I didn't know we were actually lost till just now...remember?

**LILLI.** Alright then...Aunt Bobby? What about you?

**AUNT BOBBY.** I will answer your question if...

**LILLI.** Oh no! No more deals. Your greed got us into this mess!

**AUNT BOBBY.** Fine! I will give up being a con artist and tricking people into my schemes if... you keep calling me Skipper and I can still call you first mate, Lillian.

**LILLI.** Alright then...but when we get home, I want you to give everyone their money back. And swear you won't pull me into another of one of your half-witted schemes.

**AUNT BOBBY.** But I was going to put the money toward your college fund!

**LILLI.** Really?

**AUNT BOBBY.** Sweetie, have I ever steered you wrong?

**LILLI.** Yes! Several times.

**AUNT BOBBY.** Okay, okay! I will give everyone here...a refund and I swear to never pull Lillian into one of my...half witted schemes again! (*Looks toward LILLI.*) Your turn.

**LILLI.** Do I have to?

**AUNT BOBBY.** Yes! Just this once, go along with me please!

(*LILLI reluctantly responds.*)

**LILLI.** Skipper...do you have any service on your phone?

**AUNT BOBBY.** As a matter of fact...I do! We're saved folks!

(*Group cheers.*)

**AUNT BOBBY.** Now all I have do is just start up the boat and we're out of here.

(*AUNT BOBBY tries to start up the boat but it barely starts.*)

**LILLI.** Hang on, you're doing it wrong! Let me do it!

(*LILLI tries but the boat does not start.*)

**LILLI.** Um...Aunt Bobby, did you remember to pack the spare gallon of gas?
**AUNT BOBBY.** I thought you were going to do that!

(*Group groans.*)

**LILLI.** Hey a Miss Inventor or Professor? May I call you Professor?
**INVENTOR.** You may.
**LILLI.** Would you by any chance, know how to jumpstart a motorboat with limited resources?
**INVENTOR.** I can, but it will just take a little time, but until then... we are stuck at the moment.

(*Group groans.*)

**AUNT BOBBY.** Well...at least, we're not lost at sea.
**LILLI.** Yeah, we're just stranded at sea.

## END OF PLAY

# SONIA AND NANCY

**A ten-minute play**

**By Caitlin McCommis**

## PLAYWRIGHT'S BIO

CAITLIN MCCOMMIS is a playwright from St. Louis, Missouri. She is the Ensemble Playwright-in-Residence with Tesseract Theatre where her full-length plays *You Won't See Me* and *This Is Nowhere* were produced in May 2013 and May 2014, respectively. Her ten-minute play *Fruita Sideshow* was produced as part of the Red Eye 10's Festival in September 2015. Her ten-minute play *Turtle Séance* is included in the full-length work of ten-minute plays published under the title *Mourning Hollow* by Polychoron Press. She is currently pursuing her MFA in playwriting as a member of the Playwright's Lab at Hollins University in Virginia. She is a member of the Dramatists Guild.

## SYNOPSIS

*Every woman must go unsuspected.*

Nancy is ready to quit her job working as a maid after only two months when a surprise causes her to shift her view of her boss, Sonia. It is now up to Nancy to decide if she's cut out be the person Sonia has always envisioned her to be.

## CHARACTERS

**SONIA** (f)                50's or 60's, millionaire's wife.

**NANCY** (f)                20's, Sonia's maid.

**ROBBER** (m)

## SETTING

Sonia's home.

## PRODUCTION NOTES

The setting can be as simple as needed. Sonia's wealth can be illustrated by the way she's dressed.

# SONIA AND NANCY

## By Caitlin McCommis

(*LIGHTS UP on SONIA, who is knitting. NANCY enters carrying a note.*)

**NANCY.** Excuse me, Mrs. Sonia, I was hoping I could talk to you about something this morn—

**SONIA.** I'm sorry, Nancy, now is not the time. I'm very busy.

**NANCY.** Ma'am, it will only take a moment, I really think I ought to say what it is.

**SONIA.** Do not press me when I have sharp objects in my hand, Nancy.`

**NANCY.** Ma'am I wanted to turn in my notice?

**SONIA.** Is that a question? Well I suppose you've only been here for two months. That seems to be the typical limit, you're right on schedule!

**NANCY.** I'm sorry, I just...

**SONIA.** You just what?

**NANCY.** I just never thought I'd...oh, I don't know. I imagined something different.

**SONIA.** Well I can't make much of that. What is it? Are you bored? Are you unhappy? What?

**NANCY.** Both?

**SONIA.** And why is that?

**NANCY.** I want something more... I don't know, purposeful? I knew what this job would be like, but...I didn't imagine...how it would make me feel...

**SONIA.** Speak up, Nancy. You're always carrying yourself like a mouse, I can never tell what you want.

**NANCY.** I met you and I admired your...your...

**SONIA.** Yes? My what? Speak UP!

**NANCY.** Your tenacity. But I don't feel like you respect me very much.

**SONIA.** Respect? Did I hear you say respect? Is that what this comes down to? My dear, you cannot depend on me or anyone else to feel validated. Once you learn that you will be much better off, trust me.

Perhaps you're unaccustomed to my methods. I find it takes time for most people to understand. But if you simply are not up to it...

**NANCY.** (*Looking out the window.*) It's not just that...

**SONIA.** Yes, yes, you want something with purpose.

(*NANCY is startled by something out the window. She stares for a moment, she moves back to where SONIA sits.*)

**SONIA.** I had high hopes for you when I saw the way you carved the turkey on Thanksgiving, but alas...

**NANCY.** Ma'am, were you expecting someone today?

**SONIA.** No.

**NANCY.** Well, there's a man outside. Ma'am, are you sure you're too busy? I don't think we're safe.

**SONIA.** Entirely. And if you don't mind, I'd rather you didn't stand over my shoulder.

(*SONIA continues knitting for a moment. NANCY looks back out the window. She grows more and more concerned at what she sees.*)

**NANCY.** Ma'am! Ma'am? Mrs. Sonia? I think someone's trying to get in. I've never seen him before.

**SONIA.** Is he at the front door?

**NANCY.** No, that's just it, ma'am, he's out back. I don't feel good about this.

**SONIA.** Out back? Oh good. Now listen, I know you wanted to leave, but—

**NANCY.** I'm not going out there while he's out there!

**SONIA.** Well I can see you've found your voice. Perfectly well, I could use some assistance with this.

(*Sounds of someone trying to break down a door. SONIA darts up.*)

**SONIA.** (*More excited than she should be.*) Oh how wonderful, Nancy! He's trying to break in. Now's the time, we need to take action!

**NANCY.** Ma'am, we should call the cops!

(*Sounds of broken glass offstage.*)

**SONIA.** He's in here! He got in! Okay, listen to me very closely: in the closet you will find my husband's golf clubs. Grab the Nine Iron and the Sand Wedge.

**NANCY.** A sandwich?

**SONIA.** The two with the most heft!

**NANCY.** (*Picking up SONIA's knitting needles.*) What about these?

**SONIA.** Don't be ridiculous, those are far too nice.

**NANCY.** Everything you have is nice.

**SONIA.** Nancy! The clubs!

**NANCY.** Yes, ma'am!

(*NANCY runs offstage and returns with a golf club. And a sandwich.*)

**NANCY.** Are these the ones?

**SONIA.** Very good. But what is that you have there?

**NANCY.** Is this not what you asked for?

(*A moment.*)

**SONIA.** The sand wedge, Nancy. It's another club.

(*NANCY rushes off stage and returns with another golf club.*)

**NANCY.** Where do you think he is?

(*SONIA runs towards an exit as if to look out a door.*)

**SONIA.** He's coming up the stairs.

**NANCY.** He's up here?!

**SONIA.** Shhhh. This is why we have these.

**NANCY.** Ma'am, you sound like you've done this before.

**SONIA.** Once or twice, Nancy. Millionaire's wife. Deal with this a couple times a year. Like riding a bike.

**NANCY.** How are you so calm right now?!

**SONIA.** Listen, here's what we're going to do. If he comes in here you're going to ambush him and get him on the ground. Once he's down, I'll come in with the nine iron.

**NANCY.** What if he's bigger than me?

**SONIA.** They usually are, but it shouldn't matter if you bring everything you've got. We're always stronger in the end, remember that!

**NANCY.** We're not gonna kill him, are we?

**SONIA.** Not if you do it right.

(*ROBBER enters.*)

**NANCY.** Sonia!

**SONIA.** Nancy, you're on! This is your shot!

(*NANCY freezes as ROBBER comes closer to them.*)

**SONIA.** Nancy!

(*NANCY runs toward ROBBER. He grabs the club from NANCY's hand. He shoves NANCY out of the way.*)

**SONIA.** (*To ROBBER.*) Listen, you messed with the wrong woman today.

(*SONIA beats ROBBER with the nine iron until she reaches that sweet spot where he's unconscious.*)

**NANCY.** (*More excited than she should be.*) Oh my god!

**SONIA.** I've done it once or twice.

(*SONIA grabs the sandwich and takes a bite.*)

**NANCY.** Well what about him?

**SONIA.** You'll call for the police in a moment.

**NANCY.** Yes, but should we...I don't know...tie him up or something? In case he wakes up while we're waiting for the police.

**SONIA.** My dear, we aren't in a movie. But if you really want you can go to the closet once more and grab one of the scarves.

**NANCY.** But you knitted all of those!

**SONIA.** I've knitted too many.

**NANCY.** Okay.

(*NANCY exits and returns with a scarf.*)

**SONIA.** Alright, help me with him.

(*SONIA and NANCY lift ROBBER into a chair. SONIA uses the scarf to tie ROBBER up. SONIA sits and returns to knitting.*)

**SONIA.** Would you please call the police now?
**NANCY.** Was that a question?
**SONIA.** Yes, Nancy, if you don't work for me I can't order you around.

(*NANCY exits. SONIA knits until NANCY reenters.*)

**SONIA.** Good. Now, will you stay here with us until the police arrive? Nancy, you did good work today. I appreciate your passion. It's a shame you'll be leaving.

(*SONIA puts the knitting needles down and takes another bite of the sandwich. She then offers the sandwich to NANCY.*)

**SONIA.** A bite?
**NANCY.** (*Looks to the ROBBER, then back to SONIA.*) You know you don't have to do this, right? There are devices...security measures.

(*NANCY takes the sandwich and takes a bite until it's finished.*)

**SONIA.** Yes, but where's the fun in that? Certain things are expected of a woman like me, but I'm not much for faking it when no one's watching. Would you say I put on a good show of it?
**NANCY.** From what I've seen.
**SONIA.** And you put on a show?
**NANCY.** Yes.
**SONIA.** Yes, I knew you were more than a mouse.
**NANCY.** And you're more than a—
**SONIA.** Careful now, Nancy.
**NANCY.** —Millionaire's wife.
**SONIA.** In this house we will be the ones to take control. Do you know what I did before marrying my husband? I worked. I worked day in and day out. Meeting society's expectations is wretched stuff. I'm tired of it. I wanted something that felt more authentic to me rather

than a woman of leisure. Now is my time to do what I please. A time for a new kind of leisure.

**NANCY.** This is your idea of relaxation?

**SONIA.** This is my idea of purpose. This is my time to be known by certain people for who I am, not what I am. (*To ROBBER.*) My name is Sonia! (*Beat, to NANCY.*) You remind me of myself. Are you sure you want to quit?

(*ROBBER stirs. SONIA taps him again with the nine iron so that he stops moving and loses consciousness once more.*)

**NANCY.** I don't know. Will you teach me?

**SONIA.** Teach you? I'm afraid there's more than I can cover in a matter of minutes. Who do you think I am?

**NANCY.** Sonia.

**SONIA.** I see, and you are?

**NANCY.** Nancy.

**SONIA.** Louder, please.

**NANCY.** Nancy!

**SONIA.** I don't think he can hear you.

**NANCY.** MY NAME IS NANCY! MY NAME. IS. NANCY!

**SONIA.** Beautiful. Don't shy away from it. It's in the gut. I need you to practice so you get used to it.

**NANCY.** If I stay? If I stay, will you teach me?

(*SONIA hands NANCY the knitting needles.*)

**NANCY.** Oh, no, I meant teach me how to...you know...be like you? Take control?

**SONIA.** My dear, there is more to it than that, trust me. Every woman must be unsuspected first. If you want to be in control of the situation you must first be in control of yourself. That takes concentration. Steady hands, steady mind. This isn't an absent minded task. It's a quiet control. Here, sit. Take the needles.

**NANCY.** Like this?

**SONIA.** That's perfect.

**NANCY.** How long have you been doing this?

**SONIA.** Longer than you will ever know.

(*NANCY knits. LIGHTS FADE.*)

## END OF PLAY

# SEARCH/RESCUE

**A one-act play**

**By Kimberly Patterson**

## PLAYWRIGHT'S BIO

KIMBERLY PATTERSON spent more than a decade in New York City working in Off- and Off-Off Broadway theaters in almost every capacity possible. As a playwright, her plays have appeared in the FringeNYC, the Orlando Fringe Festival, and the New York Musical Theater Festival; her musical, *Oedipus for Kids!*, is published by Samuel French and has been produced around the U.S. Kimberly is also is a participating 1MPF playwright. She lives in South Florida where she teaches high school theater and plays Japanese taiko drums.

# SYNOPSIS

*Sometimes you find everything you're looking for.*

Marianne is the daughter of Ginger La Roue, glamorous movie star, who was famously silent on the identity of Marianne's father. After Ginger's death, Marianne sets out to find him—and it's not just to have a family reunion.

## CHARACTERS

**MARIANNE** (f)                Early-mid 20s. Only daughter of movie star GINGER LA ROUE.

**THORNTON** (m)          Early 70s. An aging millionaire.

**LOLA** (f)                    Early 70s. A former actress aging gracefully. THORNTON's ex-wife.

**DENVER** (m)             Mid-late 40s. A bookish film historian from UCLA.

**BASKY** (m/f)            MARIANNE's attorney.

**SHERWOOD** (m/f)       A movie producer.

## SETTING

Present day.

## PRODUCTION NOTES

While several scenic locations are provided in stage directions, the merest hint of location would be more than sufficient. Realistic sets or massive scene changes are not necessary.

# SEARCH / RESCUE

## By Kimberly Patterson

### Scene 1

(*A funeral for a celebrity. We are indoors. MARIANNE speaks before an assembly of people.*)

**MARIANNE.** Our loss is felt not only by her friends who've gathered here today, but also by her fans around the world. Ginger La Roue was more than a movie star. She brought glamour to our lives through her acclaimed performances, and proved she was a survivor in the real-life drama of the shipwreck that thrust her into the public eye. She played so many roles both on and off screen: ingenue, sex symbol, champion of the arts, and mother. I know I can reach out to my extended family in all of the people whose lives she touched. My mother will never be gone... when I miss her, I can simply go to the movies.

(*She concludes the eulogy. THORNTON greets her warmly.*)

**THORNTON.** That was lovely, sweetheart. She would be pleased.
**MARIANNE.** Thanks.
**THORNTON.** You meet with the attorney later? You want me to come along?
**MARIANNE.** Nah, I think it'll be pretty straight-forward. But I'll call you if I think I'll need you.
**THORNTON.** Do that. Looks like the ex-Mrs. wants to come pay her respects. That's my cue to move along. Remember your mother was like family to me — and you are too.
**MARIANNE.** Thanks, Mr. Hamilton.
**THORNTON.** For god's sake, kid: Family. How about "Uncle Thornton?"
**MARIANNE.** I'll work on it.

(*He exits. LOLA enters.*)

**LOLA.** I overheard. He asked you to call him "Uncle Thornton?"

**MARIANNE.** Yeah. It's sweet. Auntie.

**LOLA.** Oh, no. Auntie Lola sounds like an aging divorcee with a mild drinking problem and a trove of attractive young men at her beck and call. Oh, actually...

**MARIANNE.** I'll stick with Lola.

**LOLA.** Your mother often called me "The Bitch."

**MARIANNE.** You knew about that?

**LOLA.** I said it right back. All in good fun, of course.

**MARIANNE.** Of course.

**LOLA.** What can I do to help you, darling? Are you having people over to the house later?

**MARIANNE.** I'm doing a small gathering with Rita and Carmen and the rest of the staff. She was so great to everyone she employed, and they loved her for it. For all her diva behavior in public, she was never a diva at home.

**LOLA.** Because she knew she was nothing without them.

**MARIANNE.** That too. And I have to meet with the attorney and then take a meeting with a producer.

**LOLA.** Why are you working on this of all days?

**MARIANNE.** Why not? It's what she would have done.

**LOLA.** You take after her so much.

**MARIANNE.** That's a compliment, right?

**LOLA.** At least I haven't started calling you "The Little Bitch."

**MARIANNE.** Thanks.

**LOLA.** Don't mention it, darling. Why I don't I call you later this week? I can help you sort through her closets... see what has value, see what fits me?

**MARIANNE.** Okay. Maybe this weekend.

**LOLA.** Take care, darling.

(*LOLA exits. MARIANNE is alone with the casket.*)

**MARIANNE.** Well, Mama, you're still making headlines. The press have been covering the story, but I wouldn't let them come in. I don't care what you thought about that; I can overrule you now. You'd've been pleased at the turn out today... most of those people actually liked you. The rest of them owed their careers to you. Yeah, you'd've been quite happy. A fitting send-off with you in the spotlight.

*(She sees a MAN in the back of the room that she doesn't recognize. He's holding two bouquets of flowers and is watching her.)*

**MARIANNE.** Excuse me? Hello, we're, um...finished? The show is over.

*(The MAN doesn't respond.)*

**MARIANNE.** I'm sorry, I don't recognize you, and this is a closed service. I think it would be best if—

*(The MAN approaches the casket. MARIANNE takes a protective step in front of it.)*

**MAN.** I didn't mean to disturb you. *(He holds out one bouquet.)* These are for your mother. She loved hibiscus flowers.
**MARIANNE.** She did...
**MAN.** *(He gives MARIANNE the other bouquet.)* And these are for you. I know this must be a difficult time.

*(The MAN turns to leave. MARIANNE's arms are now full of flowers.)*

**MARIANNE.** *(To the MAN as he exits.)* Wait! Who are you? Thank you...

*(The LIGHTS CHANGE.)*

## Scene 2

*(The attorney's office. BASKY goes over the paperwork with her.)*

**BASKY.** Her will is up to date, and you are named as the sole beneficiary of her estate.
**MARIANNE.** That seems easy enough.
**BASKY.** The house passes to you and is paid in full. You live there now, right?
**MARIANNE.** Since I was a baby.

**BASKY.** It's also likely that she has some personal property that is of significant value.

**MARIANNE.** Yeah, Mama got a lot of nice gifts.

**BASKY.** But in terms of her other liquid assets... savings accounts, investment accounts... well, she didn't have any.

**MARIANNE.** I'm not surprised. She was very "live in the now."

**BASKY.** Her active bank accounts show a balance of approximately $50,000. And she does have some credit card debt that the estate is responsible for.

**MARIANNE.** Shopping was "retail therapy."

**BASKY.** After those debts are paid—

**MARIANNE.** And after you get your cut—

**BASKY.** Yes, after the legal fees are taken out... The cash remains will be about $12,000. I don't know how that sits with you...

**MARIANNE.** Hey, that kind of money can go a long way for some people.

**BASKY.** I see here that expenses on the house... not withstanding the property tax, or the annual HOA fees which have already been paid for this year, but the regular maintenance of the grounds and the pool, plus paying the domestic staff, et cetera...

**MARIANNE.** I earn my own living. It's a very small living, but I'm sure I can cover that.

**BASKY.** Those expenses were running her about $8000 a month.

**MARIANNE.** Ah.

**BASKY.** Looking at these numbers... you're covered for the rest of July, and the next month will start on... let's see... Sunday. You'll be able to cover maintenance fees starting August?

**MARIANNE.** Sure. Some of them. Maybe. I'll be looking to cut costs.

**BASKY.** The fastest and easiest way to reduce expenses in that area would be to reduce personnel.

**MARIANNE.** I'd have to fire people? I've known some of them all my life. I don't know if I could.

**BASKY.** I understand. If there's anything I can do to help.

**MARIANNE.** Can you not charge me?

**BASKY.** I can end our meeting now, so I don't have to bill you for another ten minutes of time?

**MARIANNE.** It's a start. Thanks.

(*The LIGHTS CHANGE.*)

## Scene 3

(*A very comfortable, richly-decorated home office in the La Roue mansion. MARIANNE sits on one side of the desk; SHERWOOD sits across from her.*)

**SHERWOOD.** The plan is to start filming in a week. Obviously the studio wants us to move as quickly as possible, so they're green-lighting whatever they can.

**MARIANNE.** And what does this have to do with me, exactly?

**SHERWOOD.** We have lots of the information we need already—we have a research team working around the clock—but there are a few details that we're not able to fill in.

**MARIANNE.** I don't know what I can do.

**SHERWOOD.** Obviously you'll get some say over who will play you.

**MARIANNE.** Back up, please?

**SHERWOOD.** Your character is in the movie. Right now, it's cutting off about age 17, 18 or so. There are a lot of kids aging out of the Nickelodeon/Disney circuit that we'd like to approach... clean-cut ones, none of that Britney-Lindsay-Demi Lovato stuff.

**MARIANNE.** Huh.

**SHERWOOD.** Your mother had a few romantic links early in her career, and then had a long relationship with the director. William Mill. Then there was all that shipwreck excitement, and here you are. And she never had another serious relationship. So...

**MARIANNE.** So... ?

**SHERWOOD.** We need to know about your father. We know it's not William, the researchers have been all over that.

**MARIANNE.** He never officially came out.

**SHERWOOD.** Nobody cares about that stuff anymore.

**MARIANNE.** "Uncle" William and "Uncle" Simon had us over for Thanksgiving and Christmas every year.

**SHERWOOD.** If you give us your father's identity, it would save us time. We'd give you an "associate producer" credit.

**MARIANNE.** I can't do that.

**SHERWOOD.** Okay, we can bump that up to "executive producer."

**MARIANNE.** Don't you have to ask me permission or something before you can do any of this?

**SHERWOOD.** We're hoping you'll sign off on the life rights of your mother.

**MARIANNE.** That sounds way more complicated than what I was expecting.

**SHERWOOD.** I know this is a difficult time, and your mother's passing is still fresh—

**MARIANNE.** It was three days ago.

**SHERWOOD.** But we can't think of a better way to celebrate her and ensure that her image and talent endure...

**MARIANNE.** So you can capitalize on her death.

**SHERWOOD.** This is a trending topic. Which is why it would be mutually beneficial for you, as the representative of the estate, to give us permission to tell her story.

**MARIANNE.** And if I say no, then you can't do it.

**SHERWOOD.** The movie's getting made no matter what. It'll have to be called an "unauthorized" biopic. Ginger La Roue was a public figure, so there's nothing preventing us.

**MARIANNE.** Then it doesn't seem to matter what I say.

**SHERWOOD.** The studio feels that if we had the "authorized" biography, and were working in conjunction with her family, everything would feel more authentic and be a more valuable experience.

**MARIANNE.** You'll make more money if I say yes.

**SHERWOOD.** And you will too.

**MARIANNE.** Explain.

**SHERWOOD.** The estate would license this personal information to us for a fee. Plus, you'd have that executive producer credit on top of that, which will entitle you to about 4% of gross and we can negotiate residuals and what not. You'll probably end up in the $2-3 million range to start off.

**MARIANNE.** Holy crap.

**SHERWOOD.** I can put your attorney in touch with the studio's legal team. There'll be a pretty quick turnaround though. Thursday. We start shooting on Friday.

**MARIANNE.** That's only three days.

**SHERWOOD.** Time, as they say, is of the essence.

**MARIANNE.** I've never said that.

**SHERWOOD.** I'm sure this is a lot. How about this. Stop by the studio tomorrow... I'll show you around set, introduce to the research team, put to rest any concerns.

**MARIANNE.** My mother will only have been dead for a week.

**SHERWOOD.** The studio can offer you a quarter of a mil up front, as soon as you sign.

**MARIANNE.** $250,000?

**SHERWOOD.** Sure. If you drop off the papers in person, we'll cut you a check right there.

**MARIANNE.** On Thursday?

**SHERWOOD.** Or sooner. That depends on you.

**MARIANNE.** I can start by coming to the studio, I guess.

**SHERWOOD.** Great. And so we can get started, your father?

**MARIANNE.** What about him?

**SHERWOOD.** Can I get a name?

**MARIANNE.** Let me talk to my lawyer. I'll get back to you.

**SHERWOOD.** I'll expect you tomorrow. Don't get up—I can find my way out. It's a beautiful house you have here. I can only imagine how much work it takes to keep it going.

(*He leaves.*)

**MARIANNE.** Damn.

(*She picks up the phone and dials.*)

**MARIANNE.** (*On phone.*) Uncle Thornton?

(*LIGHTS CHANGE.*)


## Scene 4


(*Later that evening. The living room of the La Roue mansion. THORNTON and LOLA are both present, but don't sit next to each other.*)

**LOLA.** Really, darling, couldn't this have waited until tomorrow? Or at least the portion where you have to talk to me?

**THORNTON.** You can handle being in a room with me for an hour. Stop over-dramatizing. There are no cameras.

**MARIANNE.** I don't have time for your bickering. I need you to tell me who my father was.

**LOLA.** Didn't your mother ever tell you?

**MARIANNE.** She only said that his love had kept her alive during a difficult time. I assume she meant the accident.

**THORNTON.** She really should have said something.

**MARIANNE.** One of you needs to start.

**LOLA.** He seemed like a very nice young man.

**MARIANNE.** What was his name?

**THORNTON.** How much do you know about the shipwreck?

**MARIANNE.** She didn't like to talk about it, but there was plenty I could look up from the papers back then. As much as the general public.

**THORNTON.** The whole thing was a spectacular situation—if I hadn't lived it, I'd be sure that Hollywood concocted the whole thing.

**LOLA.** We're all so fortunate to even be alive. There were times we almost gave up hope of being rescued.

**THORNTON.** They were about to have the five of us declared dead... the search and rescue missions were being phased out, one by one. It was that very last one... over a month of searching.

**LOLA.** There was a freak storm.

**THORNTON.** I always felt responsible... it was my boat, my invitation.

**MARIANNE.** I read the articles. The captain's death wasn't your fault.

**THORNTON.** He really did do the best he could, and without his first mate, none of us would've made it.

**LOLA.** That boy saved our lives.

**MARIANNE.** "That boy" is my father?

**LOLA.** Let's just say she wasn't pregnant when she got on the boat that day.

**THORNTON.** You just can't imagine the panic and the realization that we were stuck and alone and had no idea how to survive. He kept us all alive.

**LOLA.** He'd been in the Navy. Knew all sorts of things about survival. We became his crew... gave us tasks to keep morale up, made sure we were taking care of the basic needs.

**THORNTON.** And companionship... that was a basic need too. We had each other. And your mother and the young man were drawn together, I suppose by circumstance.

**LOLA.** He was a sweet boy. She... what's the word? Fancied him? I don't know. I guess a disaster can make you fall in love quickly.

**THORNTON.** He certainly had his eye on her the moment she stepped aboard the boat. There was mutual attraction, and they became very good companions.

**MARIANNE.** So then what was the problem?

**LOLA.** Darling, you have to understand. We were thrown into such unusual circumstances. The things that worked there, they just didn't work the same way here.

**MARIANNE.** I think I understand the basics of "companionship" and it's pretty much the same anywhere.

**LOLA.** The rescue made her career. She went from being a perfectly adequate young actress in a sea of other perfectly adequate young actresses to becoming a Movie Star.

**MARIANNE.** But why wasn't he ever around?

**THORNTON.** Ginger made an arrangement with William, the man she was seeing. He'd moved on to Daisy Dietrich a few weeks after the disappearance, because he needed to have a woman around to protect his "identity." They allowed the press to assume that the baby was William's, but since he and Daisy were well on their way to getting married, it would've been improper for your mother to have called him out. It made her look decent... let him maintain his private life... and helped both of their careers.

**MARIANNE.** That "baby" was me, not a movie prop.

**LOLA.** You weren't a prop. She was creating a backstory and you still got to grow up knowing William and having him in your life.

**MARIANNE.** While he was very nice, I still knew he wasn't my father.

**THORNTON.** And you still turned out okay.

**MARIANNE.** But my actual father. I need to know who he is. Was? Is? I need his name.

**THORNTON.** Well, my dear, I don't know if we can help with that.

**MARIANNE.** He worked on your boat.

**THORNTON.** I paid the captain regularly for his time... In cash. And he brought his own crew. So the young man was paid from whatever I gave the captain. Whatever they worked out.

**MARIANNE.** You didn't just call him "Hey, you" and especially not while you were all stuck on an island together.

**THORNTON.** She mostly called him "dear boy."

**LOLA.** He *was* a dear boy!

**THORNTON.** He told us we could call him Gil. I honestly don't remember if he gave us a last name.

**MARIANNE.** There were no sit-around-a-campfire-and-share-stories moments?

**THORNTON.** He was from Indiana. Had a mother, father was gone. Finished high school and joined the Navy. Liked it, but was glad to be out. That was the only personal stuff we talked about.

**MARIANNE.** Are you people that superficial?!

**LOLA.** This was traumatic! We shared stories to pass the time, but too many reminders of the real world didn't make us feel better. It's a testament to us all that we came out of it alive AND sane.

**MARIANNE.** Sorry. I know. It's just... I need to find him.

**LOLA.** Why the sudden interest? You've gotten along so far. Why do you need to know so badly now? You just lost your mother.

**THORNTON.** Why not just take your time? We can help you... I'll hire you the best private eye I can.

**MARIANNE.** No. I have to do it now. Right now. Because. Because... I don't want to be an orphan.

**LOLA.** Awww, honey.

**MARIANNE.** I guess this is what I need right now as part of my healing process?

**LOLA.** Okay, then I won't press.

**THORNTON.** I wish there were more we could tell you. He really was a good guy. They were just from two different worlds.

**LOLA.** Two ships passing in the night...

**THORNTON.** That is why we're divorced.

**MARIANNE.** Fine. Thank you for your help. At least I have something more to go on. Now please both leave before you fight and get blood on my carpet.

**LOLA.** Oh god, yes. Rita will never be able to get that out.

**MARIANNE.** You'll call if you think of anything?

**THORNTON.** Of course we will. Or, I will.

**LOLA.** He's an ass. We will both call you.

**MARIANNE.** Thanks. And try to think of anything before Thursday. (*Beat.*) Grieving. You know.

**LOLA.** Right.

(*LOLA and THORNTON exit.*

*LIGHTS CHANGE.*)

## Scene 5

(*The next morning at the movie studio. SHERWOOD shows MARIANNE around.*)

**SHERWOOD.** I hope you see the love and care we want to put into the project.

**MARIANNE.** Yes, I can tell.

**SHERWOOD.** Glad to hear it. Let me introduce you to the guy handling our research... he's a film historian at UCLA, really knows his stuff. Wrote a book about the shipwreck and everything.

(*DENVER enters.*)

**DENVER.** It's not an actual book. It's my dissertation. You can't buy it at Barnes and Noble.

**SHERWOOD.** Marianne La Roue, may I present Dr. Eric Denver.

**DENVER.** I am so profoundly sorry for your loss.

**MARIANNE.** You were at my mother's funeral. You brought us flowers.

**DENVER.** Yes. I know I wasn't exactly invited. But Ginger La Roue was an important part of my life... My studies and all. I wanted to pay my respects.

**MARIANNE.** You knew about the hibiscus.

**SHERWOOD.** I told you, this guy can find just about anything.

**MARIANNE.** Did you ever meet my mother?

**DENVER.** Years ago. But scholars don't get invited to many celebrity parties.

**MARIANNE.** I suppose not.

**SHERWOOD.** I'll leave you to talk with Dr. Denver for a few minutes?

**DENVER.** Thanks. We'll be fine.

(*SHERWOOD exits.*)

**MARIANNE.** So you're the one coming up with research about my mother?

**DENVER.** She was so often in the public eye, there's no shortage of material.

**MARIANNE.** That's how she liked it.

**DENVER.** I know that Sherwood has been, I don't want to say forceful, but... forceful in getting this project moving, and I want to apologize for that.

**MARIANNE.** He was in a huge hurry to bring me here.

**DENVER.** I'm the one who asked for this meeting today.

**MARIANNE.** You did?

**DENVER.** When I heard he was going to visit you, and was asking questions about your father, I thought it might be time.

**MARIANNE.** Yeah, wouldn't want to wait until those flowers you brought had wilted first.

**DENVER.** I thought you'd want to see first-hand that we really do care about preserving your mother's legacy. All that crap he was spouting earlier, that's actually true. He just cares deeply about getting paid for it too.

**MARIANNE.** Am I allowed to see the research you've gathered so far?

**DENVER.** Of course. Everything is on the computer, but I can print you a copy. It's several hundred pages.

**MARIANNE.** How about email, then.

**DENVER.** Much better. Your email address please? Or you can just type it in there...

*(He hands her his tablet computer.)*

**DENVER.** Great. Hitting send now. Also, I want you to know that we will handle your role in the movie—your character's role—gently. It's so clear from everything I've gathered that your mother loved you very much and wanted to give you the best she could.

**MARIANNE.** She did try.

**DENVER.** It's probably hard to look at her from an outside lens, and especially as another grown woman and not just as a mother. She was truly exceptional.

**MARIANNE.** You must be good at your job.

**DENVER.** This is topic I've spent a lot of time thinking about.

*(SHERWOOD returns.)*

**SHERWOOD.** You had a good chat?

**DENVER.** I hope so.

**MARIANNE.** It was nice of you to talk to me. I'll take a look at what you've gathered.

**DENVER.** Don't hesitate to contact me if you think of any questions. You have my email address.

**SHERWOOD.** I'll walk you out.

**DENVER.** It was very nice to me you, Marianne.

**MARIANNE.** Thanks.

(*DENVER exits. MARIANNE and SHERWOOD begin to cross to a new location.*)

**SHERWOOD.** He's top-notch. Nice guy too. Don't get a whole lot of those around here.

**MARIANNE.** No, I would guess not.

(*Her cell phone pings. She checks it.*)

**MARIANNE.** Holy crap, this file is huge. It's going to take forever to read through.

**SHERWOOD.** I guarantee his work is thorough.

**MARIANNE.** We'll see. GDenver@ucla.edu. I thought you said his name was Eric?

**SHERWOOD.** I think it's a middle name. He prefers it. His first name is Gilmore... Gilbert? Something old-fashioned.

(*There is a long pause.*)

**MARIANNE.** I think I left something back in the research office. Can you take me back there?

**SHERWOOD.** Sure. I have a meeting in a few, but I can drop you off?

**MARIANNE.** Thanks.

(*They exit.*

*LIGHTS CHANGE.*)

## Scene 6

(*Back at the research office. DENVER is not present. MARIANNE waits, scrolling through the document on her phone. DENVER enters.*)

**MARIANNE.** So.

**DENVER.** I'm surprised to see you back so soon. Did you have a question?

**MARIANNE.** If you don't mind my asking... your email address says GDenver. This's going to sound strange, but would you please tell me your first name?

**DENVER.** Gilbert. Gilbert Eric Denver. PhD.

**MARIANNE.** You don't go by Gilbert?

**DENVER.** Not for a long time.

**MARIANNE.** Twenty-six years?

**DENVER.** That would be about right. Yes.

**MARIANNE.** I see.

**DENVER.** I figured you would. And it was probably time.

**MARIANNE.** Where do we go from here?

**DENVER.** I've tried so hard to distance myself from that life... make it seem academic, compartmentalize... Ginger and I fell in love on that island. Despite the terrible situation, I don't remember ever being happier. And what did I know? I was a kid. Barely 22. I was naive to think it would continue after we were rescued. Sure, we connected a few times... and I was there when her baby — you — were born... but it became clear that I wasn't right for her world. And all I wanted to do was go to college, start to make something of myself. We parted amicably, she even helped me pay for the first few years of school... but I've never loved another woman as much as I loved Ginger.

**MARIANNE.** So, what, you never tried to contact me? You knew about me all that time.

**DENVER.** She asked me not to.

**MARIANNE.** Why did you go along with it?

**DENVER.** Before the shipwreck, I was penniless... my stint in the Navy had just ended, and I was working for wealthy yacht owners to pay my way through community college. I was intent on getting an education... When we landed on that island, I almost didn't care that we weren't dead... I cared that there were no books to read.

Your mother was the only shining light in that time. When we got back, was I going to be a part of that? She knew it wasn't a life I would've chosen, and it was true. She encouraged me to stay on my own path, and I knew that she would care for you with all her heart.

**MARIANNE.** I would've rather had a father.

**DENVER.** We thought we were giving you opportunity and comfort. The best schools... the chance to do whatever you wanted with your life. Who'd want a working class kid from the Midwest intruding on your Hollywood fantasy?

**MARIANNE.** I did.

**DENVER.** If I were to have inserted myself into that life, the press would've had a field day. It would've ruined her career.

**MARIANNE.** Yes, *her* career.

**DENVER.** One thing I've learned, studying the film industry, working here... being a movie star is hard work. It's like a high-stakes poker game merged with a beauty contest. Even managing all that, do you feel like she put you second?

**MARIANNE.** Well, no. I guess not.

**DENVER.** I followed along... my research. I was never worried.

**MARIANNE.** Still, if you loved each other, you could've found a way.

**DENVER.** How much money do you think I make?

**MARIANNE.** I have no idea.

**DENVER.** Well, it's not a lot. I mean, I'm comfortable, but I've never tried raising a family on what I get paid. And it used to be a lot lower. I moved around from university to university. Never lived in one place for more than a year. You wouldn't have had a solid, stable home.

**MARIANNE.** You never got married? You don't have kids?

**DENVER.** After your mother... I lost interest in all that.

**MARIANNE.** Did you send Sherwood to ask me specifically about my father? A fact-finding mission?

**DENVER.** He is right that it would be best if we had the estate's permission to proceed. From my point of view, it would ensure that we stay honest and true to her story... otherwise, you could sue us. I made sure he knew that.

**MARIANNE.** And the part about finding my father?

**DENVER.** Maybe a little selfishness on my part. I wanted to meet you. Now that she's gone, I wanted to make sure you knew you weren't alone. Also, if we don't get official ID on the father, the studio would be free to listen to gossip and fill in the blanks. I didn't want them to suggest your real father was some... actor.

**MARIANNE.** Why didn't you just tell him who you were yourself?

**DENVER.** It wasn't my place to do so. And I didn't want for you to find out who I was in a press release. Also, it's possible that I could get fired, and they pay me much more than teaching does. I know it sounds like everyone around here is so focused on their own agenda. You think they're doing something for love, but it always comes back to money.

**MARIANNE.** Well... it's hard to separate the two. I can't say... if I were to be in a similar situation, for example... that I wouldn't let the thought of money sway me. Especially if you think you'd be doing the right thing, acting in the best interest of people who might never know.

**DENVER.** And not to get too metaphorical, but look what happens when you do try to separate love and money. Your mother and I ended up alone anyway.

(*SHERWOOD returns.*)

**SHERWOOD.** Hey, did you find what you were looking for?

**MARIANNE.** Yeah, I got it.

**SHERWOOD.** And has our Dr. Denver been using this time to continue to help champion our cause?

**MARIANNE.** He's certainly been answering a lot of my questions. I'd like to be able to talk to him again?

**DENVER.** I am at your disposal.

**SHERWOOD.** Glad to hear it. So does that mean you'll be willing to answer some of ours?

**MARIANNE.** I still have a lot of thinking to do. Can I let you both know on Thursday?

**SHERWOOD.** If that's what it takes.

**DENVER.** I've waited this long... Thursday would be fine.

(*LIGHTS CHANGE.*)

## Scene 7

(*Later that day. The living room of the La Roue mansion. As before, THORNTON and LOLA are both present, but don't sit next to each other.*)

**LOLA.** Darling, if you keep calling us over like this, I'm going to fear that you're plotting to get us back together.

**THORNTON.** That would be something to fear.

**MARIANNE.** Can I offer anyone a drink? I'm having one.

**THORNTON.** It's the middle of the afternoon.

**LOLA.** Yes, please.

**MARIANNE.** I found my father.

**LOLA.** What? How?

**MARIANNE.** Actually, he found me. Or led me to him.

**THORNTON.** Where is he?

**MARIANNE.** He teaches film history at UCLA.

**LOLA.** That's marvelous, darling!

**THORNTON.** I admit I'm thrilled. I would love to see him again. If nothing else, thank him properly for all he did to keep us alive. And to have him so close all these years!

**LOLA.** Have you spoken to him?

**MARIANNE.** Yes, actually, we met this morning.

**LOLA.** I can't believe it's all come together so quickly. It's like your mother is looking down from Heaven to bring you two together. She always was so theatrical.

**THORNTON.** And you were always so jealous. (*To MARIANNE.*) And how you do you feel about this?

**MARIANNE.** I don't know. We're grown people, with lives. I'm not suddenly going pretend every day is Father's Day. But he does seem like a good guy.

**THORNTON.** Of course. Perhaps we could all sit down together. We'd be a buffer.

**LOLA.** Do you think this will help you? You said about your grieving process...

**MARIANNE.** Well, there's more. You know that Mama was accustomed to a certain amount of luxury.

**LOLA.** Goodness, yes!

**MARIANNE.** She was prepared to pay whatever she could to keep it that way.

**THORNTON.** I never could get her to sit down with my financial guy.

**MARIANNE.** The estate is broke.

**THORNTON.** That's ok, I can help you out. How much do you need?

**MARIANNE.** No, Thornton. I don't want your money. I mean, I do, but I won't be able to just keep taking it every month?

**LOLA.** Why not? I do.

**MARIANNE.** I have to pay monthly expenses. Not like my groceries or the cable bill. I need to be able to cover paying the staff... Rita and Carmen and Joey, all of them. They're not just hired help. We're a team in this place.

**LOLA.** Also, darling, I've seen your pool boy. He is luscious.

**MARIANNE.** That's Cal. And, yeah, he kinda is.

**THORNTON.** Ladies? Could we... please?

**MARIANNE.** You know I dabble with some really small, really indie films. I make hardly any money, but it makes me happy... and now... something's come up that would provide plenty of financial security.

**LOLA.** Oh, is this that meeting you took with that producer?

**MARIANNE.** They're doing a biopic of Mama. And they're doing it, like, now. They would like me to grant them access to her life rights.

**THORNTON.** I hope you've brought your attorney into all this.

**MARIANNE.** I have, and he's looking it all over. I toured the set this morning, and it seems legit. And that's when I met Dr. Gilbert Eric Denver. He's head of their research team.

**LOLA.** Oh, the dear boy got a Ph.D! He had such a passion for learning!

**THORNTON.** So why do they need you? He's feeding the film their info... he clearly knows who he is. I'm sure he's smart enough to know he can negotiate a contract for releasing that information in exchange for compensation.

**MARIANNE.** He said he didn't want me to find out in a press release.

**THORNTON.** Yeah, Gil is a really good guy.

**MARIANNE.** If I license the life rights, the estate will get a licensing fee. A big one. And they're promising me an executive producer credit.

**THORNTON.** This all seems to make good financial sense. Hey, it might even help your career.

**MARIANNE.** Yeah, I've thought about all of that. And part of me wants to take it. It'll take the pressure off here at home. But my mother chose to never reveal it, so maybe she wouldn't want me to. And I just met him... am I ready for the whole world to get to know him before I do?

**THORNTON.** I know enough about your mother and about Gil to know that wherever they ended up after we got rescued, neither of them wanted to pretend it never happened.

**LOLA.** If she felt that way, she would've given you up for adoption or something. As delightful a child as you were, kids make this whole business more difficult. And yet she chose to have you, keep you, and love you.

**THORNTON.** I know what I'd do in this situation, but I can't tell you what to do.

**LOLA.** I can. Take the money. Get to know your father. Your mother wouldn't want you to feel like an orphan. I told you, she's looking down on you from Heaven. Meddling like always.

**MARIANNE.** I suppose in a way Gil and I were searching for each other. Now we're found.

**THORNTON.** We'll support you no matter what you decide. I'm going to get on the phone with my financial guy, let him know to expect your call. Lola, would you like me to walk you out?

**LOLA.** Thank you, but no. Today's the day the pool boy comes, and I'd like to get a good seat.

**MARIANNE.** Thanks, Uncle Thornton.

**THORNTON.** No thanks needed, sweetheart. And tell Gil we send our best.

(*He exits. LIGHTS CHANGE.*)


### Scene 8


(*The next morning. The movie studio: DENVER's office.*)

**DENVER.** And you're sure you're ready for this?

**MARIANNE.** Yes. This whole situation feels like exactly something my mother would do.

**DENVER.** There's going to be press. And it might bring William Mill back into it.

**MARIANNE.** I talked to him last night. He's the Grand Marshall of the gay pride parade in Palm Springs next year. This won't be a problem.

**DENVER.** There's still time for you to back out.

**MARIANNE.** Actually, there isn't. The money I'll get from signing will mean everything at home will keep running smoothly, but I need it in time for next month's bills.

**DENVER.** This might be a long shot, but is Rita still there?

**MARIANNE.** She is! Did you know her?

**DENVER.** Your mother and I hired her together... to be kind of a nanny for you and help out. It's part of why I knew you'd be in good hands. I'd sure love to see her again.

**MARIANNE.** Are you sure you're not going to get in trouble for this?

**DENVER.** As long as the information comes from you, it should be ok. And it's true, technically, that you never met me before yesterday.

**MARIANNE.** Here he comes.

(*SHERWOOD enters.*)

**SHERWOOD.** Well, Miss La Roue, I was certainly happy to get your phone call this morning. I hope you've got good news for me? And information?

**MARIANNE.** I spent all of last night looking at Dr. Denver's research, and it sparked a memory. Mama once told me she had a brief love affair with man who wanted to study history. I spoke with Thornton and Lola Hamilton about it, and they helped put some pieces into place.

**DENVER.** Yes, we were involved for a short time. Nothing serious came of it, but it did steer my research towards the shipwreck. A bit of personal interest informing professional interest.

**MARIANNE.** I never knew my father growing up... but I found this picture of the two of them together at the party... and I began to wonder.

**SHERWOOD.** This picture was in your research, Denver?

**DENVER.** Yes. I was always up front about the fact that I'd met Ms. La Roue. I figured that's why you hired me. I didn't think the fact that she and I had... well, you get the idea... that didn't seem relevant to my work here.

**SHERWOOD.** Eh, it is Hollywood.

**DENVER.** If you want me to step down from my position —

**SHERWOOD.** We can probably spin this to get buzz for the picture. As long as it's true. We don't want to end up with egg on our faces. Can you confirm this?

**MARIANNE.** Dr. Denver has agreed to take a paternity test this afternoon, and I'm sure the studio would be happy to "green-light" the processing. We can have the results first thing tomorrow morning. Which is Thursday.

**DENVER.** This situation is unusual, certainly, but with a positive result, the studio would have accurate information to prevent any false claims.

**MARIANNE.** As a show of good faith, I will agree to license the rights to Ginger La Roue's likeness and life story for the film, for the licensing fee that was promised in the contract.

**SHERWOOD.** Wonderful news!

**MARIANNE.** And. I will receive an executive producer credit.

**SHERWOOD.** Done.

**MARIANNE.** And. If the paternity test is a match, the studio negotiates with Dr. Denver for this info.

**SHERWOOD.** Absolutely.

(*MARIANNE shows him the signed contract.*)

**MARIANNE.** You said if I brought in the paperwork, you'd cut me a check today.

**SHERWOOD.** I did. Okay. Yes. Let me start this ball rolling. I'll gather our team. Back in a few.

(*SHERWOOD exits.*)

**MARIANNE.** Everything seems to be falling into place.

**DENVER.** It's amazing.

**MARIANNE.** Maybe after this has settled... you'd like to come to the house for dinner? Thornton wants to see you, and I'm sure Rita will. And... it would be nice to finally get to know my father.

**DENVER.** I would like that.

(*LIGHTS FADE.*)

## END OF PLAY

# FIVE STEPS TO MURDER YOUR SPOUSE

A ten-minute play

By Meghan Reimers

## PLAYWRIGHT'S BIO

MEGHAN REIMERS is pursuing an MFA in Playwriting as a member of the Playwright's Lab at Hollins University in Roanoke, VA. She holds an undergraduate degree in Dramatic Production and an MA in Theatre Arts from Bob Jones University in Greenville, SC. Currently, she works as an accompanist and theatre artist in South Carolina.

## SYNOPSIS

*It's murder on the high seas, with dolphins!*

Today's the day that Ethel will murder her husband, Richard, on a dolphin watch, but how will a sudden storm on the high seas factor in to her plan?

## CHARACTERS

**ETHEL** (f)                A millionaire.

**RICHARD** (m)         Her husband.

**STAGEHANDS** (m/f)    Non-speaking, one male, the rest any gender.

## SETTING

A boat, and a deserted island.

## PRODUCTION NOTES

The present. The world is meant to be fantastic and non-realistic.

# FIVE STEPS TO MURDER YOUR SPOUSE

## By Meghan Reimers

*(At rise, ETHEL. enters. Sound of seagulls squawking. ETHEL. holds a list.)*

**ETHEL.** It's a beautiful day! The sun is shining, the birds are singing. Today, I'm going to kill my husband. Ah, yes. There couldn't be a better day for it. Step one.

*(STAGEHANDS dressed as sailors enter and arrange the set as ETHEL watches. When they finish, they've created a boat like structure. One stagehand acts as the SKIPPER. ETHEL crosses off step one.)*

**ETHEL.** Perfect. Now for step two. Richard, here's the boat!

*(RICHARD enters. ETHEL hides her list.)*

**ETHEL.** Oh, there you are, dear. It certainly is a beautiful day for a dolphin watch, isn't it?
**RICHARD.** It certainly is.
**ETHEL.** And here's the boat!
**RICHARD.** Lovely.
**ETHEL.** I'll just purchase our tickets then.
**RICHARD.** Terrific.
**ETHEL.** One ticket for me, and one for my husband, please.

*(A STAGEHAND gives her two tickets, then ushers RICHARD and ETHEL onto the boat.)*

**RICHARD.** Oh, after you, dear.
**ETHEL.** Why, thank you. You there, Skipper thing, do give me a hand, won't you?

*(The SKIPPER salutes, and rather impressively lifts ETHEL into the boat. RICHARD follows.)*

**ETHEL.** Oh my! Hooooo! Amazing. You're very strong, aren't you? How long have you been a Skipper?

(*The SKIPPER whispers to ETHEL. RICHARD attempts to ignore this.*)

**ETHEL.** Is that so? Never mind. Shall we be off?

(*The SKIPPER goes to the back of the boat to steer. The other STAGEHANDS create the ocean around the boat.*)

**ETHEL.** Richard. Did you see that Skipper just now?
**RICHARD.** No.
**ETHEL.** He lifted me into the boat as if I weighted nothing! Which we both know is not true. It was really quite impressive.
**RICHARD.** I really didn't notice.
**ETHEL.** Oh. Let's just look at the dolphins then.
**RICHARD.** I don't see any.
**ETHEL.** Really? I see one right there!
**RICHARD.** Where?

(*ETHEL consults her list, checking off another step. RICHARD sees.*)

**RICHARD.** What have you got there?
**ETHEL.** Oh, nothing.
**RICHARD.** Let me see that.
**ETHEL.** Oh, it's really nothing.

(*He takes the list and reads it.*)

**RICHARD.** Eat breakfast, surreptitiously suggest a dolphin watch, flirt with the skipper, get him to take the list from me . . .Toss overboard. Hm. I can do that for you. (*Tossing the list overboard.*) There. Done.
**ETHEL.** Oh, I didn't mean the list, dear.
**RICHARD.** Is that right? What's going overboard then?
**ETHEL.** You, dear.

(*RICHARD laughs.*)

**ETHEL.** I'm glad you find death so amusing.

**RICHARD.** I suppose we're here for the same reason then.

**ETHEL.** What do you mean?

**RICHARD.** (*Pulling out a list.*) I have a list as well.

**ETHEL.** Is that so?

**RICHARD.** And I'm about to check off the final step.

**ETHEL.** I'm so pleased that our murderous feelings are mutual.

**RICHARD.** You don't seem surprised.

**ETHEL.** Please. I found your list two weeks ago when I spruced up our bedroom.

**RICHARD.** I see. Well, it doesn't matter now, does it?

(*He tosses his list overboard.*)

**ETHEL.** You don't know how long I've waited for this day.

**RICHARD.** I do love a good dolphin watch.

**ETHEL.** I guarantee it to be your last.

**RICHARD.** I doubt that.

**ETHEL.** Ah, but I came prepared.

**RICHARD.** Prepared? How?

(*ETHEL strikes a fighting pose. Maybe she has a sword.*)

**RICHARD.** Ah.

(*He also strikes a fighting pose, maybe pulling a sword out of a walking cane.*)

**ETHEL.** Shall we?

**RICHARD.** Indeed.

(*They begin to fight. A blinding flash of lightning, with an immediate subsonic boom of thunder.*

*Two STAGEHANDS rush in with buckets of water, and dump them on ETHEL and RICHARD. The STAGEHANDS create a storm. ETHEL and RICHARD are thrown about the boat.*)

**RICHARD.** Did you plan this too?

**ETHEL.** Of course, I did!

**RICHARD.** You can't plan the weather!

**ETHEL.** I checked the forecast!

*(They continue to fight as best they can.)*

**ETHEL.** I should have known you were only after my money when you married me.

**RICHARD.** You really think I'm that mercenary?

**ETHEL.** Am I wrong?

**RICHARD.** Yes! Although, recently, I did realize I might as well have all of your money, and none of the heartbreak. No more "millionaire and her husband."

**ETHEL.** I knew I couldn't possibly be wrong. And what do you mean, heartbreak? Is it really so difficult to be my husband? You get to play golf anytime you want.

**RICHARD.** Did you know I haven't been asked about anything but golf since you won the PGA last year?

**ETHEL.** So what?

**RICHARD.** I don't even like golf!

**ETHEL.** Oh.

**RICHARD.** You've been making assumptions about me ever since we met!

**ETHEL.** My assumptions are usually correct!

**RICHARD.** Really. And do you also assume that I enjoy being a wallflower?

**ETHEL.** I assume you're referring to my charitable events, where you drift about lackadaisically.

**RICHARD.** Do forgive me. I thought you wanted me to be ornamental.

**ETHEL.** Yes, ornamental, but not uninterested. There's a difference!

**RICHARD.** Uninterested? You think I'm uninterested?

**ETHEL.** I'll admit, they are a bit of a snooze, but you know as well as I do, those events are for brown-nosing, not hobnobbing. You can dance with anyone you want, I won't stop you.

**RICHARD.** Ethel!

**ETHEL.** What?

**RICHARD.** I don't want to dance with anyone else. I want to dance with you! I can't pretend that I enjoy watching all those pompous fat-cats holding you, when I want to be the one that holds you! If I look uninterested, it's because I'm trying not to look like a possessive swine!

**ETHEL.** Oh.

**RICHARD.** Isn't that what you want?

*(Suddenly, the STAGEHANDS [as waves] sweep the SKIPPER overboard. He exits the boat with a dramatic yelp.)*

**RICHARD.** Good lord, there goes the Skipper!

**ETHEL.** Oh my!

**RICHARD.** What are we going to do?

**ETHEL.** Not to worry!

**RICHARD.** Not to worry? No one's steering the boat!

**ETHEL.** If you'll just give me a moment.

*(She steps to the stern and begins to steer the boat. The boat pitches wildly in the storm, but ETHEL is a good pilot.)*

**RICHARD.** We won't survive this.

**ETHEL.** Oh come on, Richard. Look on the bright side! Now that the Skipper's gone, there won't be any witnesses.

**RICHARD.** Witnesses to what? Are you still planning on killing me?

**ETHEL.** Hmph. I'm not the only one on this boat that makes assumptions.

**RICHARD.** What do you mean?

**ETHEL.** There's been a change of plans, Richard.

**RICHARD.** What?

**ETHEL.** I see land.

**RICHARD.** Oh, blessed be.

**ETHEL.** We're not there yet!

*(The boat pitches violently. RICHARD is nearly thrown out of the boat. ETHEL clings to the steering wheel.)*

**ETHEL.** Richard!

**RICHARD.** What?

**ETHEL.** Help me steer!

**RICHARD.** You don't need my help!

**ETHEL.** Come here and help me anyways!

(*RICHARD joins ETHEL at the steering wheel. They steer together, ETHEL leading.*)

**ETHEL.** Why did you never ask me to dance? If you hated seeing all those "fat-cats" holding me so much.
**RICHARD.** I didn't think you wanted me to.
**ETHEL.** I married you, didn't I?
**RICHARD.** I didn't want to interfere.
**ETHEL.** But you do want to, don't you? You do want to dance with me?
**RICHARD.** Of course, I do!
**ETHEL.** That's all I ever wanted.
**RICHARD.** Then why didn't you say so?
**ETHEL.** Why didn't you?
**RICHARD.** I don't know!
**ETHEL.** Richard!
**RICHARD.** What?

(*ETHEL kisses RICHARD. The boat runs aground.*)

**ETHEL.** Oh my. We've run aground.
**RICHARD.** So we have.

(*The storm stops. ETHEL and RICHARD step out of the boat. The STAGEHANDS remove the boat, leaving ETHEL and RICHARD on the beach.*)

**RICHARD.** Where are we?
**ETHEL.** An uncharted, desert isle, I believe.
**RICHARD.** Huh. Was this on your list as well?
**ETHEL.** No. There's no list for this place.
**RICHARD.** And no charitable events, I hope.
**ETHEL.** No. But we can still dance.
**RICHARD.** Yes. We certainly can. Oh look, the sun's come out!
**ETHEL.** It's a beautiful day, isn't it?

(*ETHEL offers her hand, RICHARD takes it. They step forward together. LIGHTS OUT.*)

## END OF PLAY

# EVACUATE

**A one-act play**

**By Megan Wheelock**

## PLAYWRIGHT'S BIO

MEGAN WHEELOCK is an M.F.A candidate at The Playwrights Lab at Hollins University. Previously she attended the University of Southern Mississippi where she earned her B.A. degree in Theatre. Her motivation for writing is to help people understand a vast array of topics from all angles, and to inspire people to make a positive difference.

## SYNOPSIS

*What does it take to overcome differences?*

Seven people from seven different walks of life meet as they all seek shelter from a massive hurricane. Can they work together for their future, or will they let their differences destroy them?

## CHARACTERS

| | |
|---|---|
| **JAMES** (m) | Mid 30s male, ex-military. |
| **PETER** (m) | Early 60s male, homeless but has made the fallout shelter his home. |
| **LANCE** (m) | Late 50s male, husband to LILIAN, antique car collector. |
| **LILIAN** (f) | Mid 50s female, wife to LANCE, private tennis coach. |
| **FINN** (m) | Late 20s male, ex-military. |
| **JULIA** (f) | Late 20s female, paramedic. |
| **KAYLA** (f) | Early 20s female, college student. |

## SETTING

Toombs County, Georgia. A fallout shelter, constructed in the cold war era, that has long been forgotten about.

# EVACUATE

## By Megan Wheelock

(*At rise. On Stage Right or Stage Left there is a raised platform that is either higher or of equal height to the ceiling of the fallout shelter. It has a set of stairs leading down to the door of the fallout shelter. This platform extends past the proscenium wall into the backstage area. This is most likely where the supplies are kept that FINN brings with him. I say this because this platform is the street where he has parked his truck.*

*The fallout shelter is underground with no windows. It has a single door that leads in and out of it. The walls are made of metal, cinder blocks, and bricks. It has a look about it that tells you it was built at least fifty-five years ago. It is a bare place that has a cold harsh feeling to it. Up against the back wall are built-in shelves. Light is provided by old industrial lighting, the kind that has the metal cage around the bulb.*

*In the shadows of the room PETER's bed is set up. For what little he has it looks rather comfy. There are no luxuries only very basic necessities.*

*A hurricane is about to tear through the town. Lightning flashes, although you cannot see it from inside the shelter. There are moments when people are on the street that you can see the flashes of lightning. Thunder rumbles through the sky outside. Rain pelts the building so hard it sounds like hail or rapid gunfire beating upon the structure. The house lights begin to flicker. Lightning strikes. Thunder is heard. Rain beats harder. The house lights flicker and then go out. Howling wind is heard as the door is pushed opened.*

*JAMES, a little out of breath, enters, wearing a yellow raincoat, and a backpack slung over his shoulder. He is soaking wet from the rain. In his hand is a flashlight.*

*JAMES is trying to get his flashlight to turn on as he shuts the door.*)

**JAMES.** Come on, work dammit.

(*The flashlight finally remains on. He gets the door shut and leans his back against it taking a moment to catch his breath.*

*PETER emerges from the shadows.*)

**PETER.** Get out of my house!

(*JAMES, startled, jerks in the direction of PETER, who is coming at him with his cane in his hand ready to defend himself.*)

**JAMES.** Whoa, hey now. I'm just looking for a place out of the storm.
**PETER.** Go find your own place!
**JAMES.** I'm not here to take over. I just want a place to stay till it passes.
**PETER.** Get out!
**JAMES.** Whoa, whoa, please, I just need a safe place.
**PETER.** I don't care. That's your problem.
**JAMES.** I will die if I go back out there!

(*PETER slowly lets his guard down a little at JAMES' last words, and he lowers his cane.*)

**PETER.** Storm's picking up.
**JAMES.** Thank you. (*A small pause.*) Yeah it's getting worse.
**PETER.** You can stay till it's over.
**JAMES.** I have a few friends coming. (*Long silent pause.*) They have supplies, we will have supplies. We'll share.
**PETER.** Can always use some extra supplies.
**JAMES.** They should be here any minute
**PETER.** Just keep out of my way.
**JAMES.** We'll do the best we can. (*A small pause.*) Thank you.
**PETER.** I couldn't leave a person out in this.

(*The door opens, the storm is heard even louder. LANCE and LILIAN enter. They too are soaking wet.*)

**LILIAN.** I told you we should have left. Why couldn't you just listen to me?
**LANCE.** Stop fussing. We will be safe here.
**PETER.** (*To JAMES.*) Your friends?

**JAMES.** Um, no. I don't know these people.

(*PETER starts toward the newest intruders waving his cane angrily at them.*)

**PETER.** Get out! Get out!

(*LILIAN screams when she sees PETER coming towards them.*)

**LANCE.** Stop!
**PETER.** It's too crowded! Go away!
**LANCE.** This is a public shelter, you can't kick us out of here.
**PETER.** Wanna bet!

(*PETER goes towards LANCE. JAMES gets between to two men.*)

**JAMES.** Hey, now guys! (*To PETER.*) Can we try and work this out?

(*PETER, mumbling under his breath, lowers his cane and takes a couple of steps back.*)

**JAMES.** There is room in here. (*A small pause.*) Even when the others come.
**PETER.** No more people.
**JAMES.** We can't throw them out there in this. Even you said you couldn't.
**PETER.** This is my home!
**JAMES.** No one is kicking you out. We just want to stay here till it is safe to leave.
**PETER.** I'm not running a hotel here. (*Looks toward LILIAN and LANCE.*) Don't expect anything from me, the answer is NO!
**LANCE.** We don't want your belongings.
**PETER.** Yeah and we don't wan—
**JAMES.** (*Interrupts PETER.*) Do you need help bringing anything in?
**LANCE.** (*Indicating the suitcase.*) Everything's in here.
**JAMES.** Alright.

(*LANCE gets his phone out of his pocket and begins fiddling with it trying to make a phone call.*)

**LANCE.** Blast this damn thing. *(Holds phone up towards the ceiling.)* I'm noting getting a signal. Honey, do you have anything?

*(LILIAN rolls her eyes at him. LANCE goes over to PETER.)*

**LANCE.** Do you have a phone I could use?
**PETER.** No phone.
**LANCE.** I need a phone with a signal so that I can make a call.
**LILIAN.** What is so important that you need to call in the middle of a hurricane?
**LANCE.** I want to make sure the guys didn't forget to lock up the garage. I don't want my cars damaged.
**LILIAN.** I don't care about your stupid cars.
**LANCE.** Those are antiques. They're worth a lot of money.
**LILIAN.** Forget about the cars for a minute!!
**LANCE.** I paid a lot for those cars! I would like to know that they are safe and secured!

*(PETER and JAMES are not within earshot of LANCE and LILIAN.)*

**PETER.** *(Whispering to JAMES.)* You sure you wanna keep those two around?
**JAMES.** We're not putting them out there in this.
**PETER.** What kind of supplies are these friends of yours bringing?
**JAMES.** Canned food and water that I know of. Possibly some first aid supplies.
**PETER.** Just so we agree. It wasn't my idea to let those two stay.

*(The door opens and FINN, JULIA, and KAYLA enter.)*

**FINN.** James, you here?

*(JAMES goes over to FINN.)*

**JAMES.** You made it!
**FINN.** Yeah.
**JAMES.** Let's get the supplies unloaded.
**JULIA.** I'll give you a hand.
**KAYLA.** *(To LILIAN, LANCE and PETER.)* Let's form a line to pass the supplies down the stairs and set them up in here.

*(JULIA sets her bag down. It's a paramedic's bag full of medical/first aid supplies. The three exit back to the street. The LIGHTS DIM on the Fallout Shelter.*

*LIGHTS UP on the raised platform. FINN might be a little higher, possibly standing on a box to indicate that he is standing in the back of the truck bed as he passes out supplies for the others to carry back in. It would be best if FINN is out of sight while in the truck.*

*KAYLA, LANCE and LILIAN are outside in various spots on the stairs and by the door. PETER is just on the inside of the door.*

*The wind is blowing, lightning strikes, thunder rumbles, and the rain pours. They quickly unload two cases of water, four medium to large boxes of canned food, and five backpacks of various sizes. They do this rather quickly.)*

**FINN.** This is the last box!

*(As FINN hands the last box from the truck he picks up the last backpack and jumps out of the truck bed. They rush back inside the shelter. The lights and storm fade out as they all enter the shelter. Once the door is closed again the storm fades out completely.)*

**LILIAN.** I can't stand this place.
**PETER.** Would you rather be out there?
**LILIAN.** Don't talk to me.

*(PETER shrugs her off and walks away.)*

**LANCE.** You need to leave my wife alone.
**PETER.** I have no interest in your wife.
**LANCE.** I'm warning you.
**PETER.** You're in my home. I'm the one that allowed you to stay. So I'd watch yourself if I were you.

*(JAMES once again intervenes between the two.)*

**JAMES.** We all need to work together in this. We're going to be here for the next little bit. I know we don't all know each other but we need to try to get along. No, this is not an ideal situation. But we are all in this together now.

**LANCE.** This storm was a Cat 3 and in a matter of days it's a Cat 5, (*Stumbling for the right words and for the correct number.*) with, what, what a— (*Finally just asks.*) What was the last storm surge height they said?

**FINN.** Seventeen feet.

**JAMES.** (*Frustrated.*) It's bad. Okay. It's bad out there. We're stuck in here. So we need to just deal with it and work with what we have.

**FINN.** What do we have?

**JAMES.** I have a radio and a flashlight.

**JULIA.** I have a few medical supplies.

**PETER.** I have some blankets I can share.

**KAYLA.** I have a flashlight on my phone.

**JAMES.** (*To LILIAN and LANCE.*) What do you two have?

**LANCE.** Nothing. We didn't have much time to prepare.

(*The wind picks up outside.*)

**FINN.** (*To KAYLA.*) How much battery do you have left?

**KAYLA.** Sixty-four percent.

**FINN.** Okay great. Power it down so we can preserve what's left.

(*KAYLA turns her phone off.*)

**JAMES.** Forty-eight bottles of water. How much food?

**FINN.** I would say about four days worth. We can make that stretch if we need.

**JAMES.** What else do we have?

**FINN.** Basic gear. Waterproof matches, first aid supplies, spare batteries, flashlights and two lanterns.

**JAMES.** That's great! We'll be fine here for a few days.

**LILIAN.** Says you.

(*Hail begins to fall outside. It's heard hitting the building and sidewalk outside. Thunder is heard the rain seems to get heavier. The lights flicker a few times but stay on.*)

**JULIA.** Anybody have the time?

**LANCE.** 5:56 p.m.

**JULIA.** (*To JAMES.*) How much longer before it makes landfall?

**JAMES.** An hour or so at most by the sounds of it.

**KAYLA.** (*To PETER.*) Thanks for letting everyone stay in your home.

**PETER.** No one needs to be out in this storm.

**KAYLA.** It is very kind of you to share your home with us.

(*Suddenly the wind blows the door open.*)

**JAMES.** (*To FINN and PETER.*) Help me get the door shut.

**FINN.** (*To PETER.*) Anything we can use to jam the door with?

**PETER.** Hang on I might have something.

(*FINN helps JAMES hold the door shut. PETER rummages through the pile of junk in the corner. He returns with an old iron pipe and some old cable. The guys rig the door shut.*)

**LILIAN.** I hate this dreadful place!

(*KAYLA goes to LILIAN and tries to comfort her with a hug.*)

**LILIAN.** Don't touch me. I don't need your help.

**KAYLA.** I was just trying to be nice.

**LANCE.** The first chance we get we are leaving.

**PETER.** You know where the door is.

**LANCE.** I can't believe the police let the likes of you live here!

(*JAMES and FINN somehow manage to brace the door shut with the pipes.*)

**JAMES.** Hopefully that will hold it.

**FINN.** Everyone okay?

**LILIAN.** I will be once I am out of here.

**JAMES.** Well that might be a while.

**LILIAN.** I can't believe this day! (*To LANCE.*) I should have left without you!

**LANCE.** I didn't stop you.

**LILIAN.** Don't turn this on me.

**LANCE.** I am not turning anything on you. I'm just saying you could have left without me if you wanted to go that bad.

**LILIAN.** I hope your precious cars get blown away!

**FINN.** I am sure we all have our differences, but we're here in this fallout shelter while America as we know it is being torn to pieces by ravaging storms stretching from the West Coast to the East Coast. Nowhere is safe right now. The broadcast warnings didn't tell you this.

**LILIAN.** Lance, what is he talking about?

**LANCE.** He's just trying to scare us.

**JULIA.** (*To FINN.*) What do you mean?

**FINN.** I saw it. People started posting videos and photos all over the web. Then the signal went out. The broadcast is not covering that. You can evacuate from here but there are other storms happening. You are not safe anywhere.

**KAYLA.** I can't believe this.

**LANCE.** You're lying just to scare my wife. Just because you don't like me doesn't mean you can drag her into this.

**PETER.** If we disliked you that much, we would just put you out there to ride out the storm.

**FINN.** Look I am not making this up. (*Beat.*) When this storm has passed the world as we know it might not exist anymore.

**LANCE.** Look, that is simply not possible. Storms would not break out across the country like that. They wouldn't.

**FINN.** It's global climate change. A couple years back researchers started seeing a pattern in storm development.

**LANCE.** This global warming crap. (*Beat.*) I don't want to hear a tangent on how people are killing the Earth. Who cares? I don't. I won't be here for it so why should I worry about it!

(*The storm picks up. Thunder and lightning. The lights begin to flicker. Hail beats the ground. Howling wind and possibly the sounds of large pieces of debris being blown around outside are heard. Everyone moves closer to the center as the storm gains power. The LIGHTS FLICKER OUT. After a moment when they realize the lights will not be coming back on anytime soon. PETER speaks up.*)

**PETER.** Stay calm guys. We don't want to start bumping into each other.

(*JAMES turns on his flashlight.*)

**JAMES.** There that's better.

**PETER.** This place was built to protect us against man's nuclear weapons, this place will hold up against Mother Nature's wrath.

(*Small creaks can be heard around the upper portions of the walls.*)

**KAYLA.** I hope you're right, Pete.
**JAMES.** I think Freyja has made landfall.

(*There is a long silent pause.*)

**PETER.** (*To FINN.*) Do you have any soup in those boxes?
**FINN.** Yes, I do.
**PETER.** Break out some of those cans. I'll grab my cooking stove and pot.

(*PETER goes to his corner to grab a small camping stove and a pot for the soup. He knows the place well so he can maneuver with little to no light.*)

**FINN.** James, shine the light on the boxes, please.

(*JAMES lights FINN's path to the boxes.*)

**LILIAN.** That actually sounds nice.

(*JULIA lights the two lanterns bringing more light into the fallout shelter.*)

**KAYLA.** Comfort food?
**PETER.** You bet, and if we are all about to die, I would like to have a last meal. Even prisoners are allowed that. Maybe Mother Nature will be kind enough to let us share a meal together.

(*PETER lights the little gas camping stove. FINN brings over some cans of soup, he opens them and hands them to PETER who pours them into the pot.*

*The storm outside has gained enormous strength and the sound effects don't hold back to show this. The door struggles to open at the will of the wind. JAMES goes to the door and puts his weight against the door.*

*LILIAN gets closer to LANCE. JULIA and KAYLA find some bowls and spoons in one of the bags. JULIA hands one bowl at a time to PETER who dishes it up and passes it to FINN. FINN goes around and hands the bowls of soup to the others till everyone has a bowl. KAYLA hands out the spoons.*)

**PETER.** I'm Peter. Everyone calls me Pete.
**KAYLA.** Hi Pete, I'm Kayla.
**JAMES.** James.
**FINN.** Finn.
**LANCE.** I'm Lance and this is my wife Lilian.
**PETER.** It's always nice to eat with other people.
**JULIA.** I used to always enjoy listening to a good storm. (*Short pause.*) Until I experienced my first hurricane, that is.
**KAYLA.** I love the rain but once the thunder starts in, I hate it. Storms are so scary to me. They're unpredictable and totally uncontrollable.
**LANCE.** It's just annoying, everything about a storm is inconvenient.
**PETER.** Lance is there anything you like or, better yet, appreciate?

(*LANCE puts his food down.*)

**LANCE.** I don't like your attitude pal.
**FINN.** I'm glad we're here together and not out there alone.
**LANCE.** This isn't some pow-wow camp getaway. We need to talk about the important things going on here.
**PETER.** Like your antique car collection.
**LANCE.** I've had it up to here with you. (*Angrily shakes his hand above his head.*)
**PETER.** Look, we're in here till it passes. We can talk till we're blue in the face but the truth of the matter is that we don't know what we are going to see when we walk back out that door. If Finn is right about this, then, you won't be going back to the bed you woke up in this morning.
**FINN.** We don't know what's going to be waiting for us. So let's just enjoy this food and the company of each other.
**LILIAN.** This is such a small place for us to be trapped in.
**KAYLA.** I have family up north.

**JULIA.** I'm sure they will be fine.

**KAYLA.** I told my sister I would call her back. (*Short pause.*) That was two days ago.

**JULIA.** When this passes you can call her, it will be okay.

**PETER.** Stay positive kid.

(*The LIGHTS FADE OUT. As the storm outside reaches its peak, debris is heard being blown around. Trees are heard splintering apart. Thunder echoes through the howling winds.*

*LIGHTS UP.*

*It is silent outside.*

*Everyone is in their own spot where they stayed for the night. LANCE and LILIAN are the only ones who did not accept a blanket from PETER. JAMES is still by the door. PETER gets up and goes over to JAMES.*)

**PETER.** Hey, James. James, wake up.

(*JAMES stirs awake.*)

**JAMES.** (*Worried.*) What is it?

**PETER.** It's calm. We should go check the damage.

**JAMES.** We made it?!

**PETER.** Shhh, I don't want the others to wake up yet.

(*JAMES stands up. They quietly unblock the door and exit. LIGHTS FADE OUT.*

*LIGHTS UP on the platform.*)

**PETER.** She made it.

**JAMES.** Who?

**PETER.** Old Fallout here. She is still standing.

(*JAMES surveys the building with PETER.*)

**JAMES.** We made it.

**PETER.** Did you have doubts?

**JAMES.** I wasn't sure this place would hold up.

**PETER.** She did. (*He surveys the street.*) The rest of it is destroyed.

**JAMES.** Finn's truck is gone.

**PETER.** Well I'm sure Lance won't care about that.

**JAMES.** Let's go wake the others.

(*JAMES and PETER descend the stairs and go back in the shelter. The LIGHTS SHIFT. JAMES and PETER go around and wake everyone.*)

**KAYLA.** Is it over?

**JAMES.** Maybe.

**LILIAN.** Can we go home?

**JAMES.** We're not sure.

**LANCE.** What do you mean?

**PETER.** The shelter made it through but everything else is gone.

(*Beat.*)

**JULIA.** Gone?

**PETER.** It's bad out there.

**JAMES.** But the weather is calm.

**LANCE.** Good it's past. Lillian let's gather our things and go.

**FINN.** What time is it?

**JAMES.** Almost eight.

**FINN.** The eye of the storm passed then?

(*Beat.*)

**JAMES.** I would assume.

**KAYLA.** But.

**LILIAN.** But what? It's over. We can get out of this place.

**KAYLA.** Something just doesn't feel right.

**PETER.** No. No it does not.

**JAMES.** We could be in the eye, right now.

**JULIA.** That's insane. That would mean. (Pauses.) No, it's got to be over!

**JAMES.** I think it's something that we should consider.

**LANCE.** Come on Lilian, we need to go. I can't stand one more second trapped in here.

(*LILIAN grabs their suitcases and walks over to LANCE. She hands one to him and then they leave together.*

*LIGHTS SHIFT to the street.*)

**LILIAN.** I think they were right something seems terribly wrong.
**LANCE.** Don't let those fools get in your head. They're just trying to scare everyone.
**LILIAN.** Do you have a signal yet?

(*LANCE pulls his phone out of his pocket.*)

**LANCE.** Nothing. Dammit.
**LILIAN.** Maybe we shouldn't leave just yet.
**LANCE.** What you want to go back in there with those people?
**LILIAN.** I don't think it's safe to go home yet.

(*JAMES walks up the stairs and approaches LANCE and LILIAN.*)

**LANCE.** As fast as that wind was blowing last night the hurricane is long gone.
**JAMES.** We are going out in teams and then joining back here in an hour. You're welcome to stay until we have a better assessment of the situation.

(*FINN, PETER, KAYLA, and JULIA walk up the stairs to join JAMES.*)

**JAMES.** I'm just trying to be helpful. Look at this. Everything has been destroyed. No one knows what's beyond here.
**FINN.** You know how to get back here if you change your mind.
**LANCE.** We won't.

(*LANCE and LILIAN exit.*)

**JAMES.** Okay we should get started.

(*JAMES, KAYLA, and JULIA exit together, in the opposite direction that LANCE and LILIAN left in.*)

**FINN.** See you back here in one hour.

(*PETER and FINN exit in a different direction than the others. LIGHTS FADE OUT.*)

*One hour later: LIGHTS UP on the fallout shelter. LILIAN is trying to clean up little things that have long since been forgotten over time and have done nothing but collect dust. The door opens, rain is heard falling, wind is blowing but not that bad yet. FINN and PETER enter.*)

**PETER.** Lilian?
**FINN.** Where's Lance?
**LILIAN.** Trying to get back to the house.
**FINN.** It's not possible.
**LILIAN.** Everything is gone.
**FINN.** Did you see anybody?
**LILIAN.** No one. No one is out there!
**PETER.** The National Guard, they will be here to help.
**LILIAN.** They won't because no one is there.
**PETER.** We don't know that.
**LILIAN.** You were out there! Did you see anything? Did you?
**PETER.** One storm destroying everything. I won't believe that. I won't.

(*JAMES, KAYLA, and JULIA enter.*)

**FINN.** It's happened. There is nothing left. We have to face it.
**JULIA.** Did you find anyone?
**FINN.** No one. Nothing.
**JAMES.** Same.
**KAYLA.** What now?
**PETER.** We wait for help.
**FINN.** We need to be realistic about this. No one is coming. There is nothing left to come to. Everything is gone. You all were out there. You saw it.
**JAMES.** We need to focus.
**LILIAN.** Focus on what?

(*Thunder rumbles and the wind howls as the eye of the storm starts to pass.*)

**JAMES.** Surviving.

**JULIA.** Will this shelter hold out for another round?

**PETER.** Lance is still out there.

**JAMES.** What? Lilian, why didn't he come back with you? Where is he?

**LILIAN.** He's trying to make it home.

**JAMES.** That idiot.

**LILIAN.** He is a selfish bastard.

**JULIA.** Can we go out and get him?

**FINN.** It's too dangerous to go now.

**LILIAN.** That fool can never think of anything but his possessions.

**FINN.** (*Whispers to JAMES.*) He won't survive out there.

**JAMES.** (*Whispers to FINN.*) And we won't either if we go out after him.

(*The storm is raging once again at full force.*)

**PETER.** He's a grown man, it was his decision. He knows where this place is.

**KAYLA.** What if the roof collapses?

**PETER.** She'll hold.

**KAYLA.** I can't do this.

(*JAMES pulls FINN off to the side away from the others.*)

**PETER.** Yes, you can.

**JAMES.** (*Whispers to FINN.*) The water's only going to rise. When it happens this place is going to get flooded.

**FINN.** (*Whispering back to JAMES.*) If, if it reaches us.

**JAMES.** (*Whispering to FINN.*) We'll be trapped and drown.

**FINN.** (*Whispering to JAMES.*) No. We won't let that happen.

(*FINN looks around for something, his gaze stops on an old dusty pile of plastic sheets.*)

**FINN.** Hey Peter you know this place better than anyone, are there any cracks in the walls?

**PETER.** None that have ever been a problem.

**FINN.** Show me where. (*To JULIA.*) In my bag over there I have a roll of duct tape.

(*JULIA goes to the bag that FINN has indicated.*)

**PETER.** What are you thinking?

**FINN.** (*To LILIAN and KAYLA.*) Bring those sheets of plastic over here.

(*LILIAN and KAYLA go over to the sheets of plastic and starts shaking them out.*)

**JAMES.** The water is only going to rise. We need to slow it as best as we can.

(*Something hits the door on the outside causing a dull but loud thud.*)

**KAYLA.** (*Panicking.*) Oh God, it's not going to hold.

**JULIA.** That sounded like a person.

(*JAMES, FINN, and PETER run to the door and yank it open. Water is pouring down the stairs and starting to come inside. LANCE is lying by the door, he has fallen down the stairs.*)

**LILIAN.** Lance! (*Rushes to the door.*) Lance, are you okay?

(*The wind is blowing very hard and making it difficult for them to stand upright. PETER and JAMES manage to grab LANCE and pull him inside. KAYLA and FINN shut the door.*)

**LILIAN.** (*Frantically.*) Lance, Lance, are you okay? Honey, open your eyes! Lance.

(*LANCE is lying on the floor unconscious. His head is bleeding.*)

**JULIA.** Grab the first aid kit and some dry towels or clothes, something, anything.

(*FINN retrieves the first aid kit, while PETER finds some dry shirts for JULIA to use. JULIA notices blood coming from under him. She rolls him on his side and sees a large gash in his back.*)

**LILIAN.** Is he going to be okay?

**JULIA.** I think he made it back just in time.

(*FINN hands JULIA the first aid kit. She takes out the gauze pads and starts ripping them open.*)

**JULIA.** (*To JAMES.*) Help roll him on his side. I need to get to his back.

(*JAMES and JULIA roll LANCE onto his side. JAMES holds him in that position. JULIA gets the scissors out of the first aid kit and cuts his shirt open. She starts examining the gash.*)

**JULIA.** There's nothing left in the wound. The best we can do is clean it and bandage it. Are there any sutures or anything in there?

(*KAYLA looks through the first aid kit and pulls out a pack of butterfly bandages.*)

**KAYLA.** Only butterfly bandages.
**JULIA.** I can work with that.

(*JULIA picks up more gauze and opens it and proceeds to clean up the gash.*)

**JULIA.** Someone get me a bottle of water.

(*LILIAN quickly gets up and goes to get a water bottle. She returns and hands it to JULIA. JULIA opens it and gently pours it over the wound to wash out blood and debris.*)

**JULIA.** Hand me the alcohol wipes.

(*KAYLA grabs the wipes and hands them to JULIA. She opens them and begins wiping around the wound.*)

**JULIA.** Kayla open the butterfly strips for me, please.

(*KAYLA opens the package up and holds it out so JULIA can get one at a time. JULIA pinches the wound together with one hand and takes a butterfly bandage in the other, which she places over the wound. She does this repeatedly until the wound is closed. She uses all of the butterfly strips to close the gash on his back.)*

**JULIA.** Okay I'm going to cover it and then we can lay him on his back.

*(KAYLA hands her a couple of gauze pads and then gets the tape and scissors. JULIA covers the butterfly bandages with the gauze and then tapes the edges down.)*

**JULIA.** Okay roll him gently on his back.

*(JAMES slowly rolls LANCE onto his back.)*

**JULIA.** Let's look at his head wound.

*(PETER removes the bloody gauze so that JULIA can see the cut.)*

**PETER.** The bleeding has stopped.
**JULIA.** That's good.
**PETER.** He'll wake up with a hell of a headache though.

*(JULIA picks up an alcohol wipe and cleans the cut then puts ointment on it and covers it with a band-aid.)*

**PETER.** Let's lay him on my bed.

*(JAMES, FINN, and PETER pick LANCE up and carry him to PETER's bed. LILIAN covers him up with a blanket and sits by him.)*

**JAMES.** *(To FINN and PETER.)* Let's cover the door to try and prevent water from leaking in.

*(JAMES, FINN, and PETER go and get the plastic sheets and duct tape.)*

**FINN.** Sounds like a plan.

*(The guys start taping the plastic over the door.)*

**JAMES.** If we make it through this, our supplies are not going to last forever. How long before we can open this door again?

**PETER.** If it floods as bad as we saw about ten blocks from here, then a few weeks at least.

**FINN.** Even if we get out of here, where are we going to go for food and water? Everything has been destroyed.

**JAMES.** We'll think of something.

(*PETER helps finish taping the plastic.*)

**PETER.** There, hopefully that will help.

(*JAMES joins JULIA over by LANCE.*)

**JAMES.** How's he doing?

**JULIA.** Seems to be okay.

(*As the storm picks up strength, PETER starts walking the perimeter of the shelter inspecting the walls and ceiling for signs of impending trouble.*)

**JAMES.** (*To LILIAN.*) Anything I can do for you?

**LILIAN.** No, but thank you. He was a fool. We made it about seven blocks before I turned around. I knew there was nothing to go to even if we got past the flooding. I knew our home was gone. Everything was gone. I told him I wanted to go back. He argued with me, told me I was stupid for wanting to come back here.

**JAMES.** You did the right thing.

**LILIAN.** Thank you.

**JAMES.** I'm just glad he'll be okay.

**PETER.** Everything appears to be secure.

**KAYLA.** That's good to hear.

**PETER.** We should all settle in for the night. Not much else we can do.

(*PETER gathers the blankets and begins to hand them out.*)

**FINN.** Think anything will be left?

**JAMES.** Hard to say. You believe that storms broke out across the country?

**FINN.** Unfortunately, yes.

**JAMES.** I don't want to think this could be the end.

**FINN.** I never thought it would be the weather that took out humanity.

**JAMES.** We're the cause of all this global warming crap.

**FINN.** Yeah.

(*PETER hands JAMES and FINN each a blanket.*)

**JAMES.** (*To PETER.*) Thanks.

(*LANCE starts to wake up. LILIAN goes to his side.*)

**LILIAN.** Lance, oh thank god, you're awake.

(*JULIA goes to LANCE.*)

**JULIA.** How are you feeling?

(*LANCE tries to sit up but discovers that he is hurt.*)

**LANCE.** Ah, ow.

**JULIA.** Just lie back down.

**LANCE.** (*To LILIAN.*) I'm sorry.

**LILIAN.** Why wouldn't you just come back with me?

**LANCE.** I wanted to go home. I needed to see that our house was still standing.

**LILIAN.** But you saw. You saw what it was like out there.

**LANCE.** I did and I came back.

**JAMES.** We're glad you made it back.

**JULIA.** I closed up that gash on your back with butterfly bandages. So, you're going to need to be careful.

**LANCE.** Thank you.

**JULIA.** Glad you're okay.

**LILIAN.** You should rest.

**PETER.** We all should rest. We need to be ready to face the aftermath when this storm passes.

**KAYLA.** Agreed.

**JAMES.** Yeah.

(*Everyone settles in for the night to ride out the rest of the storm. The LIGHTS FADE OUT.*

*LIGHTS UP on the fallout shelter. JULIA is sitting by the lantern. Everyone is awake now and joining her.*)

**JULIA.** It's been awhile since I heard the wind.
**JAMES.** Should we open the door?
**FINN.** Depends. (*Small pause.*) Are we ready to see what awaits us?
**PETER.** Water hasn't leaked through the door so I don't think the flood line has reached us.
**KAYLA.** How can you be sure of that?
**PETER.** I can't be sure.
**FINN.** Do we take the chance?
**JAMES.** If we don't, we die down here.
**PETER.** Well, the inevitable will happen. It always does, just a matter of when. We open that door and get out, or we open that door and die. If we don't open that door, the supplies run out and we still die.
**LILIAN.** I say we open it.
**LANCE.** If that's what my wife wants I stand with her.
**KAYLA.** Open.
**JAMES.** I'm for it.
**FINN.** Yeah.
**PETER.** Alright then let's open that door.

(*Everyone moves to the door. JAMES and PETER remove the plastic and duct tape. PETER opens the door slowly. Water pours over the threshold. Not much but still a noticeable amount.*)

**LILIAN.** A beautiful sight.
**PETER.** That it is.
**JAMES.** Let's go out and take a better look.

(*Everyone ascends the stairs. The LIGHTS SHIFT to the street. Destruction surrounds them. The buildings that once stood are now scattered splinters and rubble. The fallout shelter is surrounded by water.*)

**JULIA.** Where do we start?
**PETER.** Anyone like fish?

**JULIA.** Fish?

**PETER.** Dinner. We need to eat. Make the supplies last as best as we can.

**KAYLA.** Where is the coast guard? Why isn't anyone here helping?

**JAMES.** We're on our own.

**PETER.** I'm going to grab my fishing pole.

**JAMES.** Let's gather some firewood.

(*PETER goes into the shelter and comes back with a fishing pole and a small tackle box. LANCE, FINN, and JAMES gather wood for a fire.*)

**LILIAN.** We will survive this even if we are the last ones.

**JULIA.** We are going to be okay.

**KAYLA.** I just don't understand why no one is here looking for survivors.

**PETER.** Because maybe we are all that's left.

(*PETER starts fishing in the floodwater. JAMES starts lighting the fire.*

*BLACKOUT.*)

### END OF PLAY

# THE SHADOW OF
# GILLIGAN'S ISLAND

**A one-act play**

**By Sean Michael McCord**

## PLAYWRIGHT'S BIO

SEAN MICHAEL MCCORD is a writer living in Charlottesville, Virginia. He studied film at UCLA and spent his twenties as a struggling screenwriter in Los Angeles before moving to New York and then crossing the Mason-Dixon line. Sean has had plays produced in Virginia, Kentucky, Colorado, California, and Stuttgart, Germany, which makes him now an internationally unknown playwright. Sean is currently pursuing his MFA in playwriting as a member of the Playwright's Lab at Hollins University.

# SYNOPSIS

Years after their rescue from Gilligan's Island, the remaining castaways find themselves drawn together by a mysterious force to perform one final journey together.

# CHARACTERS

**THE SKIPPER** (m)   Brave and true, now running a private charter after having been rescued from the desert isle some years before.

**DUNNIGAN** (m)   SKIPPER's First Mate, he harbors a secret.

**MR. HOWELL** (m)   Ostensibly a millionaire, his wealth and mannerisms may all just be an affectation as he desperately seeks a lost treasure.

**THE PROFESSOR** (m)   Once a great mind, now a form of dementia has set in and he is confined to a wheelchair.

**MARY ANN** (f)   The girl next door, resourceful and principled, she now cares for THE PROFESSOR.

**GINGER GRANT** (f)   The movie star, much like THE PROFESSOR, has lost touch with reality; she stays isolated in her movie mansion and dreams of glory days past.

**GILLIGAN** (m)   Everybody's lost little buddy, he returned to the island in secret and now lives like Robinson Crusoe, as primitive as can be.

# SETTING

The coastal town where the castaways all settled, some three hours away from the lost desert isle.

# THE SHADOW OF GILLIGAN'S ISLAND

## By Sean Michael McCord

### Scene 1

(*It is nighttime and a storm approaches a lonely wharf. Aboard a charter boat The Newton, THE SKIPPER is yelling at his first mate DUNNIGAN.*)

**SKIPPER.** Dunnigan, batten down the hatches, secure the yaw lines. The storm is coming in!
**DUNNIGAN.** Aye, Skipper!

(*A shadowed figure comes into view dockside. It is MR. HOWELL, enveloped in a long raincoat and sloping hat.*)

**HOWELL.** Skipper? Skipper, is that you?

(*SKIPPER cannot make out the figure in the dark.*)

**SKIPPER.** Who's there? Who calls?
**HOWELL.** Skipper, I have need of you.

(*The figure steps into the light and the SKIPPER finally sees who it is.*)

**SKIPPER.** Mr. Howell? Is that you?
**HOWELL.** I've been looking all over for you, Skipper. Only you can help me.
**SKIPPER.** Mr. Howell? What are you doing here? Come aboard.

(*MR. HOWELL climbs aboard. DUNNIGAN, the First Mate appears from below deck.*)

**SKIPPER.** Dunnigan, finish tying down the ship. I'll be in the Captain's cabin.

(*The SKIPPER takes MR. HOWELL by the arm and leads him out of the storm and into the Captain's cabin. HOWELL removes his rain jacket and stands revealed.*)

**SKIPPER.** That's better. I haven't seen a storm like this since...

**HOWELL.** Since that fateful three hour tour all those years ago.

**SKIPPER.** I can't believe it's you, Mr. Howell. How did you even find me?

**HOWELL.** I've been looking for you. I'll get right to the point, Skipper. I need your help.

**SKIPPER.** It is just like you to get right to the point, Mr. Howell.

**HOWELL.** What is that supposed to mean?

**SKIPPER.** It means we spent years together trapped on a desert isle, years since we escaped, years since we last spoke, and you show up only when you need my help. No "How are you doing, Skipper", or "What's new, Skipper?", or "How can I help you with my millions of dollars, Skipper?". I'll bet you don't even know my full name.

**HOWELL.** It's Jonas. Jonas Grumby. And I suppose after all this time, you may call me Thurston.

**SKIPPER.** How can I help you, Mr. Howell?

**HOWELL.** I'm sorry to be so abrupt, but the situation is dire. I need to find Gilligan.

**SKIPPER.** Gilligan? I don't know where he is. He fell off the map years ago. No one has heard from him in a long time.

**HOWELL.** It's critical, Skipper. Urgent beyond measure.

**SKIPPER.** You thought it was critical when you couldn't finish the ninth hole on your handmade golf course back on the island.

**HOWELL.** I'll admit that our behavior back then could be a bit boorish, but you must understand, Lovey and I have always been used to a certain lifestyle.

**SKIPPER.** How's Mrs. Howell?

**HOWELL.** Then you really don't know? She passed away recently.

**SKIPPER.** Oh, Mr. Howell, I wish I had known. Was she ill?

**HOWELL.** Physically she was fit as a fiddle, but her mind was never quite the same since we got back from the island. I suppose I should have seen the clues sooner. When she did go, it was very sudden.

**SKIPPER.** I'm sorry, Mr. Howell. Thanks for coming all the way out here to tell me.

**HOWELL.** My good man, no. That's not why I came. I am desperate to find Gilligan.

**SKIPPER.** Why Gilligan?

**HOWELL.** He has Lovey's will.

**SKIPPER.** What?

**HOWELL.** When we were on the island, Lovey and I filled out our last will and testament and gave it to Gilligan for safekeeping. Our departure was so hasty that neither of us gave it another thought. But then when Lovey passed away so abruptly, we realized that Gilligan has the only copy of her will.

**SKIPPER.** Mr. Howell, why on earth would you give it to Gilligan? I was the captain of the ship and the leader on the island.

**HOWELL.** Take no offense, dear man, but I am an acute observer of human behavior. Whenever there was a difficult task at hand, you assigned it to your first mate.

**SKIPPER.** Difficult task? To hold onto a will?

**HOWELL.** Not just hold onto it, Skipper. We asked Gilligan to hide the blessed thing in order to keep it safe from prying eyes.

**SKIPPER.** There's something you're not telling me, Mr. Howell.

**HOWELL.** That's all there is to it, I swear. But without a proper copy of the will, we cannot secure the estate.

**SKIPPER.** Your estate?

**HOWELL.** Despite my demeanor, Skipper, I was not born a wealthy man. I married into the Wentworth fortune. Lovey's family is the source of our affluence. Without a proper will, the entire fortune will revert to her wretched cousins and I'll see none of it again.

**SKIPPER.** I'm sorry for your trouble, Mr. Howell, but there are worse things than having to work an honest job to get by.

**HOWELL.** But it's not just me, Skipper. At the time we wrote the will, this little band of castaways was our family. Lovey was very generous to you, to Gilligan, to Ginger and all the rest. You all stand to profit handsomely.

**SKIPPER.** Even the Professor and Mary Ann?

**HOWELL.** Indubitably.

**SKIPPER.** But it's no good, Mr. Howell. Even if we could find Gilligan, and no one has heard from him for years, we left all that behind when we escaped.

**HOWELL.** But how far could he have gone? Surely someone in our little band of castaways has heard from him?

**SKIPPER.** Mary Ann has been taking care of the Professor. I suppose I could drop by and ask if they've heard anything.

**HOWELL.** Capitol idea, Skipper.

**SKIPPER.** If I help you, Mr. Howell, I do it for all of us. The Professor is not doing well. He and Mary Ann are just getting by, and I've invested everything I had into this charter boat

**HOWELL.** What of Ginger?

**SKIPPER.** The last I heard, she was living in her movie mansion and not returning anyone's calls. Maybe she'd respond to you.

**HOWELL.** Very well, Skipper. I will seek out Miss Ginger Grant while you call on Mary Ann and the Professor.

*(The SKIPPER considers this for a moment, then calls in his first mate.)*

**SKIPPER.** Dunnigan?

*(DUNNIGAN appears in the cabin.)*

**DUNNIGAN.** Aye, Skipper?

**SKIPPER.** I'll be going ashore with our visitor. Keep *The Newton* ship-shape and ready to sail.

**DUNNIGAN.** Aye, Skipper. We'll be ready to shove off.

**SKIPPER.** Thanks, little buddy. And Mr. Howell...

**HOWELL.** Yes, Skipper?

**SKIPPER.** I really am sorry to hear about your wife. It's sad to think that we will never be all together again, but if Mrs. Howell's will can make everyone's life a little easier, I'll do what I can to help.

*(Unseen by the others, DUNNIGAN is very interested to hear about the will.)*

## Scene 2

*(A split stage. On one side is THE PROFESSOR's library, stacked high with old books and dusty tomes. The years have not been kind to THE PROFESSOR. A form of dementia has set in and he is confined to a wheelchair. MARY ANN, his faithful companion of many years, tends to his needs as the storm rages outside.*

*On the other side of the stage, and miles away, is the well-appointed mansion of GINGER GRANT. She sits alone in the semi-dark, her features occasionally illuminated by flashes of lightning.)*

**PROFESSOR.** The storm! No, not the storm!

**MARY ANN.** It's all right, Professor. It's just a little weather.

**PROFESSOR.** A three-hour tour.

**MARY ANN.** That was a long time ago, Professor. We're home now.

**PROFESSOR.** Home?

**MARY ANN.** Yes, we're safe. On dry land.

(*Thunder crashes outside, and rain can be heard pelting down.*)

**MARY ANN.** Well, mostly dry. The Skipper called. He's on his way over.

(*The LIGHTS COME UP on GINGER's side of the stage. She has been sitting in a wingback chair, staring into the darkness. A pair of loud knocks are heard on both sides of the stage.*

*MARY ANN goes to answer her door. Simultaneously, GINGER gets up to answer her door.*

*The SKIPPER enters on MARY ANN's side.*)

**MARY ANN.** Skipper!

**SKIPPER.** It's good to see you, Mary Ann.

(*At the same time, GINGER opens her door and MR. HOWELL appears on her threshold.*)

**HOWELL.** Ginger. How are you, my dear?

(*Without a word, GINGER glides back to her chair and sits down. Not sure what else to do, MR. HOWELL comes in and closes the door behind him as the storm rages outside.*)

**MARY ANN.** I was happy to hear from you, Skipper, but a little surprised that you would call on us so late in the day.

**SKIPPER.** I have news, Mary Ann.

(*Meanwhile, MR. HOWELL sits down next to GINGER.*)

**HOWELL.** Ginger, you look splendid, as always. A real movie star.

(*GINGER does not respond. HOWELL takes in his surroundings. The mansion reeks of old money and untended dreams.*)

**HOWELL.** You ... seem to be doing well for yourself. Well, at one time anyway.

**MARY ANN.** What is it, Skipper?

**SKIPPER.** I'm sorry to tell you this, but Mrs. Howell passed away recently.

**MARY ANN.** Oh, that's too bad. Was she ill?

**SKIPPER.** From what Mr. Howell told me, her condition was a lot like the Professor's.

**HOWELL.** Ginger, say something.

(*GINGER slowly turns, as if she is just noticing her visitor.*)

**GINGER.** Who are you? Did my agent send you?

**HOWELL.** Your agent? Ginger, it's me, Thurston Howell the third.

**GINGER.** I'm ready for my interview.

**SKIPPER.** How is he, Mary Ann?

**MARY ANN.** He has good days and bad days. But lately, mainly bad days. He seemed to take a real turn after Gilligan left here.

**SKIPPER.** Gilligan? Here? How long ago was that?

**MARY ANN.** We lose track of time in this place. I don't get out very often. A year ago? No, two at least. Maybe more.

**HOWELL.** Interview? Ginger...? Why yes, I'm here to interview you. About the island.

**GINGER.** Who sent you? I have left strict instructions that I will not talk about that place.

**HOWELL.** The Skipper sent me.

**GINGER.** Skipper?

**HOWELL.** Yes. We're looking for Gilligan. Do you know how to find him?

**SKIPPER.** This may be the last place Gilligan was seen. Do you know what became of him?

**MARY ANN.** He spoke to the Professor, I don't know what about, then he left.

**GINGER.** (*Sparks up with interest.*) Oh, Gilligan! The funny little man.

**HOWELL.** Yes, that's Gilligan.

**GINGER.** From the television.

**SKIPPER.** Professor, it's me, Skipper. From *The Minnow*.

**PROFESSOR.** The Minnow would be lost. The Minnow would be lost.

**HOWELL.** What? No, not from the television. From the island.

**GINGER.** Do you know that I once did an island picture with Richard Chamberlain?

**MARY ANN.** He gets upset talking about Gilligan.

**SKIPPER.** I'm sorry Mary Ann, I have to do this. Professor, where did he go? Where's Gilligan?

(*THE PROFESSOR looks at Skipper, really looks at him, then pulls him in close.*)

**PROFESSOR.** (*Sotto voce*). The storm!

(*The lightning flashes, the thunder roars. GINGER  hears it too. She and THE PROFESSOR speak simultaneously.*)

**GINGER / PROFESSOR.** 4, 8, 15, 16, 23, 42...

**MARY ANN.** He said the same thing to Gilligan.

**HOWELL.** It's hopeless, utterly hopeless.

**SKIPPER.** What does it mean?

**MARY ANN.** I have an idea, but it doesn't make much sense.

**SKIPPER.** Show me.

(*MARY ANN retrieves a dusty old atlas from the PROFESSOR's shelves.*)

**MARY ANN.** After Gilligan left, I noticed that this had been opened. Turn to page four. (*She shows the SKIPPER.*)

**SKIPPER.** Why, this in an old atlas. And there on page four is our original point of departure.

**HOWELL.** Is that a phone number? Your measurements? No, that wouldn't be right.

**SKIPPER.** Let's turn to page eight. Look at that, we can draw a line from page four to page eight. Say we hit the storm there and it blew us southeast, that would take us to (*Turning pages.*)... Yes! Page fifteen and across sixteen to twenty-three and ending up on ... forty-two!

**HOWELL.** Wait, coordinates. Like on a map. That's it!

**MARY ANN.** And that's where it stops making sense. There's nothing on that page but miles of ocean in every direction.

**HOWELL.** And who knows maps better than that salty old sea dog himself, the Skipper!

**SKIPPER.** But that's it, Mary Ann! Our island doesn't appear on any maps. It must be somewhere on this page. If we can get close enough, and the Professor's old radio is still broadcasting, we might be able to find the island.

**MARY ANN.** Find the island? Why would you do that?

**SKIPPER.** There's something on the island that Mr. Howell wants. I don't know if he's being truthful with me, but I also want answers about what's happening to us.

**MARY ANN.** What do you mean?

**SKIPPER.** Do you get those dreams too, Mary Ann? Do you hear the island calling to you, especially during storms?

(*The lightning flashes and the thunder rolls one last time. GINGER and THE PROFESSOR avert their eyes as if seeing something they cannot bear. MARY ANN also responds, but shakes it off.*)

**MARY ANN.** I thought ... I thought maybe it was the Professor's madness affecting me.

**SKIPPER.** I hear it too. I think we all do. This madness is getting to all of us. Mrs. Howell was the first to fall.

**HOWELL.** Ginger, you're coming with me.

**GINGER.** Coming with you? To an audition?

**HOWELL.** Yes, my dear. A big audition. We'll go see, *erm* .... Mr. DeMille!

**GINGER.** I'm ready.

(*MR. HOWELL leads GINGER out of her mansion.*)

**SKIPPER.** Come with me, Mary Ann, and bring the Professor. This is no way to live. If what Mr. Howell says is true, and if we can find Gilligan, then all of us can have a better life. What do you say?

**MARY ANN.** (*Considers the PROFESSOR.*) I don't know if he's ready to travel.

**SKIPPER.** I can't do it without you, Mary Ann. Anyway, I don't know if I'd want to. And the Professor can't get by without you. It's your choice, but I think that we should all be together.

**MARY ANN.** (*Speaks to the PROFESSOR.*) Professor, Skipper is here. He wants to take us away from this place. He wants to find Gilligan. Can you do that?
**PROFESSOR.** Gilligan?
**MARY ANN.** Yes.
**PROFESSOR.** The storm.
**MARY ANN.** What about the storm?
**PROFESSOR.** It stopped.

(*MARY ANN and the SKIPPER pause and listen. There is no more thunder or lightning. They look at each other.*)

**SKIPPER.** It's time.
**PROFESSOR.** I'm ready.

(*SKIPPER and MARY ANN bundle up THE PROFESSOR in blankets and wheel him out.*)


### Scene 3


(*On the deck of* The Newton. *DUNNIGAN has the helm. SKIPPER comes up from below deck.*)

**DUNNIGAN.** How are the passengers, Captain?
**SKIPPER.** Please, call me Skipper, little buddy. And it's a bit rough down there. Mr. Howell seems to have the worst of it. Steady as she goes.
**DUNNIGAN.** Skipper, I'm picking something up on the radio.
**SKIPPER.** Let me listen...

(*SKIPPER picks up the headset and hears the familiar instrumental strain of the Gilligan's Island theme song.*)

**SKIPPER.** That's it! That was the only tape we had, so the Professor put it on a loop. Follow that sea shanty, helmsman.
**DUNNIGAN.** Aye, aye, Skipper!

## Scene 4

(*Morning. The Newton bobs gently in an island inlet. GINGER is lost in thought. MARY ANN tends to THE PROFESSOR. MR. HOWELL emerges from the boat and stumbles out onto the beach.*)

**HOWELL.** Land. Blessed land.

(*DUNNIGAN emerges from the brush.*)

**DUNNIGAN.** Good morning, Mr. Howell. Feeling any better?
**HOWELL.** Who are you again?
**DUNNIGAN.** Dunnigan, sir. First mate aboard *The Newton.*

(*The SKIPPER appears, his usual chipper self.*)

**SKIPPER.** Top of the morning, Mr. Howell. We had a rough night, but we're here.
**HOWELL.** And where is here?
**SKIPPER.** Look around. Don't you recognize it?

(*MR. HOWELL does just that, and it dawns on him.*)

**HOWELL.** We're here? The island?
**GINGER.** Skipper, is it true?
**SKIPPER.** I spotted our old encampment just over that ridge.
**HOWELL.** Ginger, you seem ... lucid.
**GINGER.** I don't remember much about how we got here, but yes, I'm all right.
**HOWELL.** And you, Professor? Are you well?
**PROFESSOR.** Like I woke up from a long dream.
**HOWELL.** Remarkable.
**SKIPPER.** Dunnigan and I are going to start carrying supplies to the camp. Who's with us?
**GINGER.** I want to go.
**SKIPPER.** Mary Ann?
**MARY ANN.** I should stay here with the Professor until we can figure out how to get his chair over the ridge.
**PROFESSOR.** That won't be necessary.

(*THE PROFESSOR pulls himself up out of his chair. Everyone gasps.*)

**PROFESSOR.** I think that I will walk.

(*MARY ANN rushes to his side.*)

**MARY ANN.** Professor!
**PROFESSOR.** I'm all right. A little wobbly, but I can make it.

(*THE SKIPPER comes to the other side of THE PROFESSOR and they all excitedly make their way into the brush.*)

## Scene 5

(*The castaway's settlement. Bamboo huts, odd machinery built out of reeds and palm fronds. It is old, but surprisingly still intact, as though someone had been tending but not repairing it.*

*SKIPPER, MR. HOWELL, and DUNNIGAN emerge into the clearing first.*)

**HOWELL.** Good job, Skipper. Capital.
**DUNNIGAN.** This is how you lived?
**SKIPPER.** Like Robinson Crusoe.
**DUNNIGAN.** How did you make it work?

(*SKIPPER and MR. HOWELL pause. This is a big moment for them.*)

**HOWELL.** We were family.
**SKIPPER.** Yeah, we were.
**HOWELL.** Thank you, Jonas.
**SKIPPER.** You're welcome, Thurston.

(*MARY ANN, GINGER, and THE PROFESSOR join them. They are all awed by what they see.*)

**MARY ANN.** I can't believe that this is all still here.

**GINGER.** It's just like we left it.

**PROFESSOR.** Once I get up to speed, I can begin repairs.

**DUNNIGAN.** Repairs? I don't understand. Are you all staying?

(*Everyone stops. They look at each other with a combination of confusion and resolution. None had ever fully discussed this, yet somehow everyone was thinking the same thing.*)

**HOWELL.** Well, no, that would be ludicrous, right? We're just ... excited to see the old camp and we want to put things in ship shape. Isn't that right, Skipper?

**SKIPPER.** Yes, that's right. Ship shape.

**DUNNIGAN.** I thought you all came here to retrieve something?

(*SKIPPER looks at MR. HOWELL, but before he has a chance to say anything, GINGER lets out a scream. Everyone turns to look.*)

**MARY ANN.** Ginger, what is it?

**GINGER.** These ... these scarecrows! They startled me.

(*They look around and notice their likenesses scattered around the camp, human figures made of reeds and grass and stuffed into clothing to look like the castaways.*)

**HOWELL.** Let me see. Why, this looks like you, Skipper.

(*Indeed, they have found a straw man stuffed into a crude replica of khakis, a blue shirt, and a seaman's hat. Similarly, MARY ANN spots a svelte straw figure lovingly packed into an evening gown.*)

**MARY ANN.** And here you are, Ginger.

(*The castaways look around the camp and continue to find their crude lookalikes.*)

**PROFESSOR.** I found ... me!

**MARY ANN.** I found you, Mr. Howell. Oh, and ... Mrs. Howell.

**HOWELL.** Lovey?

**MARY ANN.** And she's holding a box.

**HOWELL.** Let me see that!

(*HOWELL rushes over to the straw Howells but SKIPPER blocks the way.*)

**SKIPPER.** What's in the box, Mary Ann?
**MARY ANN.** Why, it's jewels. Lots of them!
**SKIPPER.** You told me we came to find Mrs. Howell's last will.
**HOWELL.** In a way. It was her last will that these jewels should go to me.

(*HOWELL wrests the box away from MARY ANN.*)

**HOWELL.** These are worth a fortune. We couldn't very well tell everyone what we had. We were trying to hide them away from Lovey's dreadful family, the Wentworths.

(*DUNNIGAN pulls out a gun and levels it at MR. HOWELL.*)

**DUNNIGAN.** (*Affected accent.*). And now the Wentworths will take them back.

(*Again, everyone gasps.*)

**SKIPPER.** Dunnigan? What's going on here?
**PROFESSOR.** You're name isn't actually Dunnigan, is it?
**DUNNIGAN.** No, it's Miller Wentworth.
**HOWELL.** Little Millie?
**DUNNIGAN.** Hello, Uncle Thirsty.
**HOWELL.** But you're just a child!
**DUNNIGAN.** Not anymore. I grew up hearing the family stories of the great Thurston Howell the third and how he married our Aunt Eunice and absconded with the family fortune. I found Captain Grumby here, served as his first mate for years, learned everything about how to pilot a boat, even put up with him calling me "little buddy", all for the day you would show up and lead us back to the island and that very box. Now you must hand it over to me.

(*THE PROFESSOR has been sneaking up on him. DUNNIGAN sees and fires his gun at the straw duplicate of THE PROFESSOR, blowing its melon head off. THE PROFESSOR stops.*)

**SKIPPER.** You better do what he says, Mr. Howell. It's not worth it.

(*Painfully, agonizingly, HOWELL hands the box over to DUNNIGAN.*)

**SKIPPER.** What's your plan, Dunnigan. Are you just going to strand us here?

**DUNNIGAN.** You're not fooling anyone, "Skipper". This is where you wanted to be all along.

(*Suddenly, a wild, long-haired, bearded man comes screaming out of the brush and jumps on DUNNIGAN, knocking him down to the ground.*

*It is GILLIGAN.*)

**GILLIGAN.** You shot the Professor! You shot him!

(*THE PROFESSOR, the real Professor, jumps in and pulls GILLIGAN off while the SKIPPER and MR. HOWELL restrain the now disarmed DUNNIGAN.*)

**PROFESSOR.** Stop it! That's enough! No more violence.

**GILLIGAN.** Professor? You can talk? But I saw him blow your head off.

**PROFESSOR.** That wasn't me, that was just some scarecrow. Hold on ... Gilligan?

**SKIPPER.** Gilligan!

**GILLIGAN.** Skipper? You can talk too?

**SKIPPER.** Gilligan, it's us. All of us. We're really here.

(*GILLIGAN stares at the SKIPPER, then slowly looks around the camp and spots the rest of the castaways.*)

**GILLIGAN.** All of you? You're really here? Really, actually here?

(*Everyone rushes over to GILLIGAN. There is much rejoicing. Unfortunately, they've all forgotten DUNNIGAN, who now retrieves his gun and picks up the box of jewels.*)

**DUNNIGAN.** So now everyone has what they want. Skipper, you've got your "little buddy" back, you've all returned to your precious island, and I've got the Wentworth family fortune.

**GINGER.** Dunnigan ... I mean, Miller Wentworth. Those jewels would look just fabulous on me.

**DUNNIGAN.** Stow it, movie star. I'm on to your moves and I assure you that they won't work on me.

**HOWELL.** Never mind, Ginger, it's all right. Take the jewels, Millie. May they bring you the happiness that you seek. Nothing you do now will take away the fortune that I already had with your Aunt Lovey.

(*DUNNIGAN backs away slowly, then dives into the brush and away. Slowly, the castaways exhale.*)

**GilLIGAN.** What just happened?

**SKIPPER.** It doesn't matter, little buddy. What matters is that we're all back here together.

(*MR. HOWELL is eyeing the straw dummy of Mrs. Howell.*)

**HOWELL.** Most of us, anyway.

**SKIPPER.** Are you okay, Mr. Howell?

**HOWELL.** Splendid, Skipper. Thank you for asking. He was right, you know. This is where we all wanted to be.

**PROFESSOR.** I postulate that something about the environment of the island affected our central nervous system, and leaving here precipitated something akin to withdrawal. It may be that we will need to spend the rest of our natural lives here.

**HOWELL.** In that case, we should get right to work. Ginger, would you accompany me to the back nine? I believe I left some bamboo drivers there. That golf game isn't going to finish itself.

**GINGER.** I hope I have the proper shoes.

(*MR. HOWELL and GINGER wander off.*)

**PROFESSOR.** I should get right to work on repairing the weather station. Mary Ann, would you help me?

**MARY ANN.** Of course, Professor.

(*MARY ANN and THE PROFESSOR go off to work together.*)

**SKIPPER.** Well, little buddy, let's get you cleaned up. I'm sure we can find a razor and a red shirt.
**GILLIGAN.** Skipper, I have a boat of my own on the other side of the island.
**SKIPPER.** That's good to know, Gilligan. But you heard the Professor, we're not going anywhere.

(*GILLIGAN and the SKIPPER go in search of a razor.*)

**GILLIGAN.** I still can't believe that you're all here. But I'm glad you showed up when you did, Skipper. I was running out of reeds to stuff into your dummy.

(*SKIPPER playfully hits GILLIGAN with his hat.*)

**GIILIGAN.** Okay, I believe, I believe...!

## END OF PLAY

# THE ISLE

**A one-act play**

**By Kyle Philip Jackola**

## PLAYWRIGHT'S BIO

KYLE PHILIP JACKOLA is a wandering theatre artist and freelance writer based primarily in Western North Carolina, and a current MFA playwright in The Playwrights Lab at Hollins University. When not in school, Kyle works at the Brevard Music Center in Brevard, North Carolina as a staff production assistant where he has done everything from orchestral stage managing to technical stage rigging. Most recently his work has been been performed in the 2016 RedEye 10s International Play Festival, Centerpiece Reading Series in Roanoke, VA, The Hollins 2016 Playwright's Festival, Brevard College, and around various basements and backyard firepits up and down the east coast. He has a BA in English and Creative Writing from Brevard College.

## SYNOPSIS

*"We are such stuff that dreams are made of..."*

Gil and Sarah Jane find themselves trapped on a small deserted island with only themselves and a mysterious painted volleyball for company. Will they make a new life for themselves on the island, or will the memories from the past keep them from connecting with each other?

## CHARACTERS

**GIL** (m)                    20s-40s, male. A man who just wants something familiar.

**SARAH JANE** (f)             20s-40s, female. A woman making the best of her situation.

## SETTING

A very tiny island. The entire thing should be about the size of a living room.

## TIME

Present

## PRODUCTION NOTES

The less realistic the staging, the better.

# THE ISLE

## By Kyle Philip Jackola

### Scene 1

(*A tempest! A dinghy! GIL is fighting with the oars of the boat. Across from him is SARAH JANE wearing a life preserver. A giant wave washes over them. Another, and another...*)

**GIL.** Boatswain!
**SARAH JANE.** Who?
**GIL.** Good, speak to the mariners: fall to't yarely, or we run ourselves agroud. Bestir, bestir!
**SARAH JANE.** It's only me and you, Gil!

(*GIL looks around.*)

**GIL.** Heigh, my hearts! Cheerly cheerly, my hearts!
**SARAH JANE.** For God's sake— English, Gil!

(*A pause*)

**GIL.** We're going down!
**BOTH.** Ahhhhhhhhhhhhhhhhh!!
**SARAH JANE.** Abandon ship!
**GIL.** All lost! To prayers to prayers! All lost!

(*They jump over board. LIGHTS FADE TO BLACK.*)

## Scene 2

*(GIL sits on a deserted beach staring out at sea.)*

**GIL.** *(Silence.)*

*(A wave. It washes over GIL as he sits. The wave recedes and we see that WILSON [from "Castaway"] and a large FedEx box has washed up on shore. GIL picks up ball and box.)*

**GIL.** Say, what's in the package, Wilbur? *(As WILSON.)* "I don't know, Gil! But I do know it's a federal crime to open someone else's mail!"

*(SARAH JANE enters.)*

**SARAH JANE.** Just open it, Gilly. I'm starvin'!
**GIL.** Sorry, Wilbur *(As WILSON.)* "Wait, Gil! Think about what you're doing!" *(As GIL.)* Lady's orders...

*(GIL punts WILSON back into the ocean. He and SARAH JANE open the FedEx box. It contains a single Dolly Parton wig. GIL tries it on. SARAH JANE stares at him.)*

**GIL.** What?

*(SARAH JANE shakes her head and exits.*

*WILSON washes back on shore. GIL takes off wig and goes to put it on WILSON. He looks admirably at his work, then exits. LIGHTS FADE.)*

## Scene 3

(*GIL digs in the sand. He discovers a conch shell. He blows into it. SARAH JANE enters. She looks around for the sound, confused.*)

**SARAH JANE.** I thought I heard something.

(*GIL shrugs. SARAH JANE shrugs. SARAH JANE exits. GIL blows again. SARAH JANE reemerges.*)

**SARAH JANE.** Did you not hear that?
**GIL.** What?
**SARAH JANE.** Nevermind.

(*SARAH JANE exits. GIL blows again. SARAH JANE races in.*)

**SARAH JANE.** Just then!
**GIL.** What?
**SARAH JANE.** The sound!

(*GIL shakes his head. SARAH JANE leers a moment, then exits. GIL blows again. Nothing. Again. Nothing. Again. SARAH JANE approaches from opposite side and sees the conch. GIL begins to blow again, but SARAH JANE takes the conch. She exits. GIL resumes digging. He discovers a comically large conch shell. BLACKOUT.*)

## Scene 4

(*A bright and sunny afternoon. WILSON lays on a mat of palm leaves hooked up to primitive, nonfunctional coconut heart monitors, and an improvised wooden lightning rod. GIL has constructed a body for WILSON made out of tree branches and leaves, and has made a coconut bikini to clothe his creation. WILSON is wearing the Dolly Parton wig. GIL makes thunder and lightning noises.*)

**GIL.** (*Stereotypical mad scientist.*) My creation!

(*GIL makes WILSON lift his head as if he's looking around.*)

**GIL.** It's...*ALIVE!* Mwahahahahahahahahahaha!!!!

(*SARAH JANE enters. She sees WILSON and takes his head. The wig falls off.*)

**GIL.** Wait! I need that!
**SARAH JANE.** Sorry, Gilly. Soccer practice.
**GIL.** Who am I supposed to play with now?
**SARAH JANE.** You can come along if you want.

(*GIL looks at her.*)

**GIL.** No thanks.
**SARAH JANE.** Fine, suit yourself.

(*SARAH JANE exits with WILSON. GIL picks up wig and exits. LIGHT CHANGE.*)

## Scene 5

(*GIL and WILSON in wig on the beach. GIL pulls out a bottle of wine, a wheel of cheese, and a knife.*)

**GIL.** More wine?
**WILSON.** (*Moved and voiced by GIL.*)  Simply divine!

(*GIL pours.*)

**GIL.** More cheese?
**WILSON.** Ooooooo, yes please!
**GIL.** (*Slices cheese.*) What's playing for tonight's main feature?

(*GIL holds up a water-logged VHS box of the movie "Titanic."*)

**GIL.** This was all I could find in the dinghy...
**WILSON.** "Titanic." Sounds familiar. What's it about?
**GIL.** Beats me...

(*They both shrug. GIL pulls out a remote and aims it at an unseen television.*

*SFX: "I'm flying Jack!  I'm flying" from "Titanic." They snuggle close. SARAH JANE enters behind them unseen. GIL has his arm around WILSON. SARAH JANE watches a bit longer, then exits.*)

**GIL.** You hear something, little buddy?
**WILSON.** (*Shakes head no.*)
**GIL.** Hmmmm...

(*They continue watching. The LIGHTS FADE TO BLACK.*)

## Scene 6

(*SARAH JANE on stage doing a magic routine. She shows the audience a large empty crate, then closes it. She taps it once with a pineapple, then opens it again. A pineapple has appeared inside the crate. She takes it out and closes it again. She taps on it with a life-preserver ring. She opens it again and a life preserver ring has appeared. She takes it out and closes it again. She pulls out a cardboard cutout of Leonardo DiCaprio as Jack from "Titanic" and taps the crate. She excitedly opens the crate. GIL steps out buckling his pants like he's just finished using the rest room. He turns.*)

**GIL.** All yours!

(*SARAH JANE breaks the cardboard cutout over her knee in frustration and storms off.*

*GIL shrugs and exits opposite direction. LIGHTS CHANGE.*)

## Scene 7

(*GIL is kicking WILSON into the waves. The waves bring WILSON back to GIL every time. SARAH JANE enters. GIL doesn't see her.*)

**SARAH JANE.** Hey!  Gil!

(*GIL misses his kick. He looks at SARAH JANE.*)

**SARAH JANE.** Sorry...

(*He lines up to kick again. He kicks WILSON farther than he's kicked before.*)

**SARAH JANE.** Woah! That's past the breakers!

(*GIL smiles. They wait for WILSON to return. Nothing...*)

**SARAH JANE.** Is he...(*WILSON floating farther away from land*)?
**GIL.** Wilbur?

(*GIL runs to the edge to the tide.*)

**GIL.** Wilbur!!  Come back!!  Wilbur!!

(*He falls to his knees...*)

**GIL.** *Wiiiiiiiiiiiiiiiiiillllbuuuuuuuuuuuuuuuurrr!!*

(*He sobs. SARAH JANE approaches him. He turns, hugs her around the waist, and cries as the tide comes in on both of them. LIGHTS FADE TO BLACK.*)

## Scene 8

(*GIL sits on the beach staring at the waves wearing the Dolly Parton wig.*)

**GIL.** (*Silence.*)

(*A FedEx box falls from above and hits him in the side of the head. He picks it up, inspects it, looks around for where it could have come from, then opens it. It's a coconut painted like WILSON. SARAH JANE enters. Her hair is teased up like the Dolly Parton wig. She sits down next to GIL. He looks at her. She looks at him. She pulls out the conch shell and blows it. He smiles, pulls out his comically large conch shell and blows back. They blow their conch shells together. They stop and stare at each other. Sunset. SARAH JANE rests her head on GIL's shoulder. Their hair gets stuck together. They pull apart and laugh. SARAH JANE blows the shell. GIL blows his shell. He puts his arm around SARAH JANE and they cuddle. She blows the shell once more. WILSON rolls on stage next to the coconut. LIGHTS FADE.*)

### Scene 9

*(GIL stands in front of other castaways in a solemn down light. Wearing a costume made entirely of leaves and mud.)*

**GIL.**
Now my charms are all overthrown,
And what strength I have's mine own,
Which is most faint: now, 'tis true,
I must be here confined by you,
Or sent to Naples. Let me not,
Since I have my dukedom got
And pardon'd the deceiver, dwell
In this bare island by your spell;
But release me from my bands
With the help of your good hands:
Gentle breath of yours my sails
Must fill, or else my project fails,
Which was to please. Now I want
Spirits to enforce, art to enchant,
And my ending is despair,
Unless I be relieved by prayer,
Which pierces so that it assaults
Mercy itself and frees all faults.
As you from crimes would pardon'd be,
Let your indulgence set me free.

*(SARAH JANE erupts in applause. GIL bows. SARAH JANE comes up to GIL and hands him a bouquet of clams. She brings WILSON and COCONUT CHANNEL, both wearing Dolly Parton wigs, to GIL. He kisses WILSON and COCONUT CHANNEL on the cheeks then turns and kisses SARAH JANE. LIGHTS FADE.)*

### END OF PLAY

## Horrible Shakespeare: A Mini Musical

Book and Lyrics by Sean Abley
Music and Lyrics by Ryan O'Connell

Musical
Short 30 minutes Cast - 21 either

A student field trip to Shakespeare's Globe Theatre in London takes a horrible turn...literally! In this 30-minute musical, a nameless tour guide leads the students into the sub-sub-sub basement of the theater, which houses the Horrible Productions of Shakespeare's Plays Museum. Each exhibit magically transports the tour group into the world of a truly wretched production of some of Shakespeare's most famous works - "Romeo Mime vs. Clown Juliet," "Santa Hamlet," "Macbeth's Burgers," "Taming of the Real, Live Shrew" and "Twelfth Night of the Living Dead." This musical is perfect for festivals with time restrictions, in-class performances, or as one half of an evening of one-acts. Sheet music, demo tracks and performance karaoke tracks also available.

www.ingramcontent.com/pod-product-compliance
Lightning Source LLC
LaVergne TN
LVHW051409080426
835508LV00022B/3003